T0161229

HEALING
WITH
ENTACTOGENS

Therapist and Patient Perspectives on
MDMA-Assisted Group Psychotherapy

Torsten Passie, M.D.

Foreword by Ralph Metzner, Ph.D.

Multidisciplinary Association for Psychedelic Studies (MAPS)

100% of the profits from the sale of this book will be used to
fund psychedelic and medical marijuana research and education.

Healing With Entactogens
ISBN 0-9798622-7-2
ISBN-13 978-0-9798622-7-4
Copyright 2012 by Torsten Passie, M.D.

This is an extended and revised English translation of
Heilungsprozesse im veränderten Bewusstsein
(Berlin, Germany: VWB Publishers, 2009).

Book & cover design: Mark Plummer
Text set in Futura

Printed in the United States of America by McNaughton & Gunn, Saline, MI

HEALING
WITH
ENTACTOGENS

Therapist and Patient Perspectives on MDMA-Assisted Group Psychotherapy

Dedication

This book is dedicated to
Werner Middendorf, M.D.,
a great teacher and friend

Acknowledgements

Many thanks to Thomas Duerst, Dipl. Psych., for his diploma thesis on which this work is partially based, and to Professor Rolf Verres, M.D., of the University of Heidelberg in Germany, who unintentionally promoted the publication of this work on a broader scale. I am thankful to Professor John H. Halpern of Harvard Medical School and Linnae Ponté of MAPS for carefully editing the manuscript. Steady support for this unusual work came over the last decades from Professor Hinderk M. Emrich, M.D., Ph.D., at the Hannover Medical School in Germany, and Rick Doblin, Ph.D., of MAPS.

The future might teach us to exercise a direct influence,
by means of particular chemical substances,
on the amounts of energy and their distribution in
the mental apparatus. It may be that there are other
still undreamed-of possibilities of therapy.

—S. Freud (1938)

Contents

Foreword

by Ralph Metzner, Ph.D.

During the 1980s, MDMA, which was originally explored as an effective adjunct to psychotherapy with remarkable anxiety-reducing effects and minimal if any visual or cognitive alterations, escaped out of the offices of a few dozen psychotherapists in the U.S. and Europe, and became the recreational party drug ecstasy, consumed by thousands at all-night rave-dance events. Predictably, as the Ecstasy-fueled rave subculture grew in numbers, laws were passed in all relevant countries making possession of the drug illegal and thereby largely unavailable to therapists to use in their practice—even those (like myself) who had previously used it with good results.

This story was an almost exact replay of the story of how LSD was introduced into the culture in the 1960s: At first, reports from psychiatric researchers showing dramatic evidence of its effectiveness as an adjunct to psycholytic therapy in a range of conditions, including alcoholism, various forms of neurosis, as well as the stimulation of religious experiences and the enhancement of creativity. Then, after enthusiastic reports from the therapists who themselves experienced it and its availability in the underground market, the therapy drug LSD became the "acid" of long dance parties with light shows and psychedelic rock music, and was subsequently made illegal and therefore unavailable to established medical-psychiatric researchers.

Now, another generation later, the mainstream culture seems to be opening up again to the therapeutic possibilities of these substances (and others such as DMT, ibogaine, and ayahuasca,) and serious research on possible applications is again being done in the U.S. and in Europe as well as Israel. In the meantime, there is a flourishing underground culture in which thousands of people experiment with psychedelic substances on their own accord and create cultural artifacts (books, music, and art) inspired by them. This paradoxical situation was highlighted at a recent MAPS conference, in which a presenter asked how many people had participated as a subject in a psychedelic research project and about a half dozen people raised their hands; when he asked how many people had themselves experienced psychedelics, virtually the entire audience raised their hands.

Torsten Passie, a German psychiatrist working at the Hannover Medical School in Germany, is a leading researcher in this field and has done several studies on the therapeutic applications of psycholytic (or psychedelic) drugs. In this book he presents his research findings on the therapeutic possibilities of MDMA, with MDE and LSD also considered in a minor way. It is a qualitative research study, in which his data are the experience reports and interviews from individual and group psycholytic therapy sessions.

He reports that the primary findings are a marked reduction of anxiety, along with physical relaxation and the ability to think calmly about one's emotions and interpersonal difficulties, making connections and producing acceptance and understanding. These results basically confirm the observations from several earlier published studies with MDMA in psychiatric populations. They are also consistent with the reports from a wide range of people that I collected in a book I edited and published in the mid-1980s called *Through the Gateway of the Heart*, under the pseudonym that I used at that time (Sophia Adamson).

I want to say a word here about terminology. Torsten Passie, who is a friend as well as a colleague of mine, uses the word "entactogen" to describe the class of drugs like MDMA whose primary neuropsychological action is a marked decrease of interpersonal and intrapsychic fear—thereby facilitating a seemingly effortless reintegration of previously defended traumatic memories and perceptions. This is in marked contrast to the primary effect of the classical psychedelics (e.g., LSD, mescaline, and psilocybin,) which involve visual and affective amplification of all psychic contents and processes, including fear—thereby making difficult or "hellish" trips much more likely than with MDMA (where they are virtually absent). "Entactogen"[o] means something like "touching within," or getting in touch with one's own inner processes.

In a friendly debate I had with several of my colleagues in the pages of the MAPS Bulletin (Vol. 4, No. 2., Summer 1993), I suggested that "touching within" doesn't really distinguish the MDMA-type experience from the LSD-type experience. My own preferred term for these substances (and the experience they can facilitate) is empathogenic—generating a state of empathy, both empathy with others and empathy with one's own self in past or present conflict situations. This to me is the basis for the heightened affective understanding—the integration of emotion and reasoning consequent upon the absence of fear and anxiety—that Dr. Passie's study demonstrates.

If there is one complaint I have about his presentation in this study, it is the lack of attention paid to empathy. In the treatment of trauma, which is one of the main and most promising applications of MDMA-therapy, it is the ability to consider the effects and impacts of the traumatizing event in one's life calmly and without fear. In such experiences, it is as if the remembered fear is recognizably there, associated with the recalled events, but sotto voce: not overwhelming or paralyzing. Considering the central and essential role that empathy plays in the therapeutic process, I think one (thus far) underestimated important application of MDMA is in the training of psychotherapists—for whom the ability to experience and authentically express empathy is crucial.

Torsten Passie's research not only deals with the amplified psychotherapy possible with MDMA, but also with the neurophysiological and neurochemical correlates of the experience. His observations and conclusions here are particularly insightful. He states, on the basis of his studies, that MDMA deactivates the amygdala (the seat of fear-rage emotional reactivity) and reciprocally activates prefrontal brain circuits (which underlie calm thinking). This is the neurophysiological counterpart to the empathic understanding of self and others reported by the patients. There is also a massive release of serotonin, the neurotransmitter associated with a non-depressive, non-fearful attitude.

To my mind the most provocative of his findings is that MDMA results in a massive release of prolactin, the hormone associated with breast-feeding, and oxytocin, sometimes called the "cuddle hormone." Both of these hormones are released during nonsexual post-orgasmic intimacy. As Dr. Passie points out, this release of nonsexual intimacy hormones correlates perfectly with the often-remarked subjective experience of MDMA-users—that they feel intimate with others, wanting to touch and be physically close, but not sexually aroused. Even couples that were intimately involved have reported that with MDMA, the sexual drive is often just not there.

Being nonsexually but emotionally intimate with another human being is not a very common experience, particularly with men (though women who are mothers obviously do know it from the infant bonding situation). It is, however, a supremely useful kind of connection to cultivate in a therapeutic situation, including for the therapist, where the slightest hint of sexual interest is likely to set off all kinds of alarm signals in both therapist and patient. (This is not to advocate for the use of MDMA by the therapist in the therapy, but rather for its use in the training of therapists.)

This is a unique aspect of MDMA that contributes to what Dr. Passie calls its "astonishing efficacy in enhancing psychotherapeutic communication." Or, as one of his therapy patients reported, "you don't have a wall around yourself anymore. It's not that you take it down—it just isn't there." His book deserves to take its place as an essential milestone in the integration of MDMA-type drugs into psychotherapy practice.

—RM

Introduction

Psychoactive substances, such as the hallucinogens LSD and psilocybin, or entactogens such as methylenedioxymethamphetamine (MDMA) or methylenedioxyethylamphetamine (MDE), could be helpful psychotherapy tools, especially in the practice of psychodynamic and trauma psychotherapy (Mithoefer et al. 2011, Winkelman and Roberts 2007, Abramson 1967). These therapeutic options were the object of extensive research in the 1950s and 1960s (cf. Passie 1997). The substances in question were discredited and banned towards the end of the 1960s. Since the early 1990s, research has been reinitiated to make use of these substances in psychotherapy and other medical applications. More-recent efforts were made possible thanks to a new group of psychoactive substances, the so-called entactogens, which, compared to classic hallucinogens like LSD, are more clinically manageable and open up new types of therapeutic possibilities.

Approaches for using these substances in a psychotherapeutic framework were defined during the early 1960s. The term "psycholytic" was coined in 1960 by the English psychotherapist Ronald Sandison at a conference about LSD-assisted therapy (Barolin 1961). Psycholytic can be translated as "soul-loosening." This new term was unanimously accepted by the European LSD therapists, introduced in the Oxford English Dictionary, and is still in use today. The term essentially refers to the fact that these substances (in low to medium dosages) can activate psychological processes and make unconscious material (e. g., memories and conflicts) accessible for psychotherapeutic processing and typically lead to intense re-living and release of emotions. In general, "psycholytic" may also be an appropriate term to describe the effects of the newer entactogenic substances. A newer alternative term for this kind of therapy is "substance-assisted psychotherapy" (cf. Jungaberle et al. 2008).

Presently, no systematic description has been offered of the entactogens' psychotherapeutic mechanisms and effects. In the pages to follow, we isolate and describe the elements or mechanisms responsible for the entactogens' therapeutic effects. Such effects only partially overlap with those found in treatments with hallucinogens (as established by Leuner 1971 and Grof 1980). Therefore, entactogen-assisted psychotherapy deserves its own clear presentation.

Before its prohibition in 1986, psychotherapists in the USA were using MDMA as an adjunct to psychotherapy (Greer and Tolbert 1990, Stolaroff 1997, Widmer

1997). Just before it was made illegal, a number of these psychotherapists intervened at the U.S. Drug Enforcement Administration (DEA) and drew attention to the unique psychotherapeutic potential of MDMA (Seymour 1986). This led to a DEA Administrative Law Judge (ALJ) court case, which reviewed the banning of the substance and resulted in a recommendation that MDMA continue to be available legally to therapists and psychiatrists. In the end, the Administrator of the DEA rejected the ALJ's recommendation. Nevertheless, evidence supporting MDMA's potential as a therapeutic adjunct was so strong that the World Health Organization (WHO) Expert Committee on Drug Dependence, which recommended that the recreational use of MDMA be banned around the world, also provided the following statement supporting research in addition to the declaration of prohibition:

> It should be noted that the expert Committee held extensive discussions concerning the reported therapeutic usefulness of 3,4-methylenedioxy-methamphetamine. While the expert committee found the reports intriguing, it felt that the studies lacked the appropriate methodological design necessary to ascertain the reliability of the observations. There was, however, sufficient interest expressed to recommend that investigations be encouraged to follow up these preliminary findings. To that end, the Expert Committee urged countries to use the provisions of article 7 of the Convention on Psychotropic Substances to facilitate research on this interesting substance (WHO Expert Committee on Drug Dependence 1985, p. 25).

Attempts to use entactogens therapeutically never stopped after MDMA was banned. Greer and Tolbert's early work (1986) is exemplary, and therapy has continued with the Swiss Physician Society for Psycholytic Therapy (SÄPT) (Styk 1994, Benz 1989). In 1986, when MDMA was prohibited, an organization was founded called the Multidisciplinary Association for Psychedelic Studies (MAPS). MAPS develops and funds a renewal of research into the risks and benefits of psychedelic drugs, especially the therapeutic effects of the entactogen MDMA. MAPS' long-term goal is to develop MDMA into an FDA-approved prescription medicine for posttraumatic stress disorder (PTSD) and eventually other indications as well. Research is gaining traction with studies on MDMA-assisted psychotherapy for posttraumatic stress disorder by Michael Mithoefer (2008, Mithoefer et al. 2011) in the USA and Peter Oehen (2008) in Switzerland. In addition, a study has started at Harvard Medical School's McLean Hospital to evaluate anxiety reduction from MDMA-assisted psychotherapy in advanced-stage cancer patients (Halpern 2008).

The author of this work considers the various work groups named above as close colleagues. In addition to formal training as a physician and psychiatrist, training and clinical work with Hanscarl Leuner and other psycholytic therapists provides an additional basis for the contributions of this book.

Framework of the psycholytic sessions

In the group therapy treatments that will be the focus of this booklet, medium-range doses of MDE (125-150 mg p.o.), MDMA (100-125 mg p.o.), or LSD (75-150 μg p.o.) were administered. The treatment was carried out using the principles of the psycholytic method (Leuner 1971, Fontana 1965) during weekend seminars with 8 to 15 patients in two treatment rooms. Prior to a weekend treatment, numerous individual non-drug therapy sessions (10-30) took place between the patients and therapists in the spirit of psychodynamic psychotherapy to sensitize for introspecting one's own inner psychological processes and their dynamics.

The psycholytic sessions were carried out with three permanently present professional psychotherapists (two male, one female). Patients used eyeshades during portions of their psycholytic sessions and soft background music was played through headphones to smoothly stimulate experiences. Participants were told to freely give themselves up to their inner experiences as much as possible. Immediately preceding substance ingestion, participants were instructed to discuss their current personal issues with one other participant, in order to channel group as well as individual focus upon meaningful therapeutic aspects of the seminar (see Appendix 2 for more details of this therapeutic procedure). Throughout sessions, patients were offered help from the therapists present, if the therapists felt that it could be helpful or necessary. Group interpretation and integration meetings took place the following morning after a psycholytic session (Dürst 2006) and patients would then resume their normal psychotherapeutic treatment.

All patients interviewed had between 5 and 10 psycholytic sessions. Most sessions took place with entactogens (MDMA or MDE), while LSD-sessions made up only around 10% of the total. In this respect, the following discussions or interviews refer nearly all to the effect of entactogens.

The patients treated were male and female patients with character, anxiety, and sexual neuroses as well as neurotic depressions and psychosomatic disorders. Practically all those treated had a high level of social function and none had previously received in-patient psychiatric or in-patient psychotherapeutic treatment (Dürst 2006).

Psychotherapeutic experiences with entactogens

The following presentation is based on semi-structured interviews, each lasting approximately two hours, with six former patients who underwent psycholytic therapy for an average of two years (for more details see Appendix 1 and Dürst 2006). The ways things were encountered and the content of experiences under the effects of entactogens are presented as examples as they occurred within a constant, stable therapeutic framework.

Using the phenomenological method (cf. Moustakas 1994), we investigated which elements our patients experienced as particularly impressive, helpful, and effective in solving their problems during their therapy with entactogens, in order to gain insight into their therapeutic effects and mechanisms. The elements involved are presented in Table 1.

Framework of the psycholytic sessions

1. Focusing on issues

2. Group experience

3. Significance of therapists

4. Degree of control over the drug experience

Elements of therapeutic processing

1. Decrease of anxiety, enhanced opening up, and building of trust

2. Psychophysical relaxation and altered perception of one's body

3. Acceleration of psychological processes

4. Regression

5. Rescripting of past behaviors or events

6. Problem actualization and corrective new experiences

7. Transpersonal experiences

Integration and therapeutic changes

1. The process of integration

2. Therapeutic results from the patient's perspective

3. Comparisons with conventional psychotherapy

Table 1: Overview of the elements of the experience gained in psycholytic therapy with entactogens

The points named in the overview are presented below and explained based on statements from the interviews. Where not otherwise given, the page references refer to work done by Dürst (2006). The interview texts, which were originally recorded on tape and then transcribed verbatim, were lightly edited only to improve reading, syntax, and grammar. They were not edited for content. Where more than two words have been taken out, put in, or changed, this is marked by "..." or "[ ]".

Framework of the psycholytic sessions

1. Focusing on issues

The therapy took place, as mentioned before, in a group setting, which included focusing on the topics of therapeutic importance upon arrival for the treatment session. Participants were put in pairs to report on their current situation in life and biographical events that particularly interested them as topics at that time. Each participant spoke for 10 minutes without interruption while the other listened, whereupon the roles were reversed. In a following round with all participants, each reported on that which he or she had identified and concentrated upon as the focus subject. In addition to the participants getting to know each other, this served to further reinforce their individual issue or the questions arising from it.

> "For me it was important to identify my subject in concrete terms. Well then the therapist, while I somehow meant that and that is my issue, mostly put his finger on it. That was important on the evening before. I then often realized what my issue is. Often I had somehow such chaos in my head or thought I had another issue and then the therapist recognized that my issue was a quite different one. That was very helpful...." (16)

2. Group experience

The therapy groups were made up of 10 to 15 participants. Some participants knew each other from earlier sessions. Because almost all participants were in individual depth-psychology treatment during the period that they participated in the psycholytic sessions, the group sessions were a new experience which mobilized many fears and desires.

> "The group was very important for me because there were different sorts of men and women there. Because of this, you could live out particular roles. You see yourself in this state, reflected in the other people or roles, for example as father and mother or in roles which you experience every day, such as colleagues at work, etc. You can really get stuck into it if you want. And above all, it was important to listen to the other reactions, to swap stories. Also during the sessions, for me it was great to see, 'How do the others see me, how do they see that?'" (66)

"At one sitting, I felt dislike of a person and then stood above this feeling and felt, 'What is it with me? What is it I dislike?' Another time, I suddenly understood all the men who were there. I knew exactly what was going on in them. I could suddenly register all their male problems. In another sitting, during the welcoming, I saw a great amount of evil in one person, who presented himself quite well and as conformed. That led me to understand that who one professes to be is not that—who one really is. Since then I look much deeper into people and can feel them better..." (14 f.)

"To be integrated into a group was one of the most important occurrences for me. For the first time to experience what I am scared of—how coy I am and how full of complexes. Normally one appears as a person with a purpose, like at work. However, here you present yourself as a person, nothing more. No job with which you can create an image for yourself. You are simply there with that which you are, nothing more. That was attached to very much fear at the beginning." (42)

"The events in the group were also very important because one was deeply confronted by oneself there but was at the same time in the group and could immediately put that into practice. Because you had opened yourself, had dared to open yourself and a group was there, which was also willing to accept you, you could practice the new feeling immediately. And those were very good and helpful, also constructive contacts. You learned from one another..." (35)

"At the end of the group sessions, discussions took place, and at night you were together and could talk. Then the threat was gone. That was really important for me, that I do not find people a threat in the first place anymore but instead can build up trust, in particular to groups, which I do not control. I used to be together with groups before, but then I always controlled the groups. And here I had the feeling, 'I can let go of the control.' I can really relax. Nothing happens to me, there is good will. It is a really important experience, which continues in my life, because I can again show people trust." (28)

"You are very close to one another, but during the journey you are by yourself...but then, if you then need access to the people, they are there and you simply share. I find that wonderful, to be able to share, without finding your fulfillment in the others. The limits are there. It isn't that you invade one another or ask for too much intimacy. Absolutely not. It is simply just right, as it happens, not too much and not too little, and you also have the possibility at all times to regulate that. Really I have never experienced that there were any arguments because someone had gone too far or the like..." (42/43)

"Special encounters crop up with individual participants as well as general support felt from the group...that was my greatest worry during the journey. I had asked my therapist, 'Will people be able to approach me?' That is something I do not want. That already says a lot about my fears. Of course someone came up to me immediately, but that was no problem at all because care is taken that one is not disturbed. That means it never happens without the okay from the therapist. They pay good attention to this. In addition I could also say when I did not want to. There were not many, but there were a couple of contacts which were unbelievable, which played a great role for me." (38)

In these examples, it becomes clear that in groups like this, a whole spectrum of anxieties and reservations are mobilized in the realm of interpersonal relations and respective previous biographical experiences. In exactly the same way that these issues of relation are activated, new encounters of a correcting nature and experiences which foster trust are made possible. Due to the anxiety-reducing effect of entactogens, anxieties that usually get in the way can be overcome and new, more positive experiences achieved which often counteract negative memories and fears. It is also interesting that the group processes do not devolve into a sense of chaos, which might be expected considering the great differences in individual entactogen experiences. Rather, it appears that auto-regulative processes are more at play, which (extended through the structure and guidance by the therapists) hold the group, to a large extent, in an undisturbed equilibrium. This is also confirmed by results from Spencer (1963), Fontana (1965), and the Swiss psycholytic therapists (see Gasser 1996).

It appears that the anxiety-reducing effects of entactogens make possible an accelerated and deeply trustful submission to therapeutically effective occurrences within a group setting.

3. Significance of therapists
In principle, the relationship with one's psychotherapist within any psychotherapy is of central significance. However, the therapist steps into the background in support of his/her patients' involvement in their inner "psycholytic" processes that will autonomously play out during an entactogen-augmented sitting. As such, it is important to present examples that illustrate how the significance of the relationship with the therapist is retained along with the therapist's unique responsibilities that may arise within entactogen-assisted treatment.

"The therapist's manner was really quite important in order to create the correct combination of behavior to loosen up, warm up, and initiate social behavior and, on the other hand, allow everyone to also remain centered on oneself. I found the latter a very good aspect that one did not sit all cuddled up together too much like a group of brooding hens. Like, 14 people in a hayloft, really close. Along the lines of, 'we are all poor little children together, and we really, really like each other.' That would have just diverted attention. He did that very well, creating this balance, which on the one hand made clear that everyone ought to attend to his problems and issues and that a symbiotic melting with one another would not help the cause...that was an art...something for which I really admired him for..." (56)

"In that moment, when you had inwardly freed yourself from wrong and frightening thoughts...it was there that he passed on an atmosphere of courageousness in the face of supposed horror...as if a lion trainer were there, one who, if such a beast comes into the cage, says, 'Okay, it's a lion, let's have a look at him then.' This way of dealing with the frightening feelings was very important." (56)

"I find it quite important that a female and male therapist are present. In particular, if there is a difficulty there, such as with me with the parents, the divorce etc.—the therapists play an important role. Because if you fetch help in the changed condition and talk to them, they can then exemplary embody the mother or the father for you. That was quite important for me...meaning that the therapists always played that through with me. In that way the woman is just as important as the man. There were issues, for example, if you discover your feminine side, which you would naturally talk over with a female person rather than with a man...." (68)

"In the first sessions, I always had the feeling that the therapists had to rescue me out of my situation. So...that is how I used them. But I was also mistrustful towards the therapists and always thought that they are also definitely somehow not right. But that was my problem, being mistrustful. Later I needed them, to have someone to point in the right direction or to talk with, to find solutions, in order to understand myself. Sometimes I also misused them, as a raised finger in warning, if they criticized or told me off because I was a pain, wanted too much, or I played with them." (16)

"The therapists...were deeply human, unbelievably understanding, but nevertheless also very critical... To communicate like that with a person is simply unbelievable. Before I had this experience, I did not think it possible that one can be so close to someone and nevertheless not put demands on them like a person you love... You simply feel you are taken seriously, accepted, and understood, but also taken seriously in the sense that you can never say anything which will always only be answered with "yes," but will be answered critically, and also lovingly." (37)

"In contrast to the single sessions, the therapist played an almost decentralized, peripheral role during the group sessions. He was very important in the introductory phase, for the trust which I had summoned up, for the jump into this water... He was very important for me in his role as somebody who created this setting, this atmosphere. During the session itself he played almost no role for me. I can only remember one, two, three times, where I called him in as someone very well versed in all my problems, to whom I just had to tell what I had found out..." (56)

It is clear from these descriptions that the desires, perceptions, and occurrences connected to the therapists pertain to a number of factors. The therapists are in a general sense wanted and experienced as individuals who create a trusting and safe structure. In addition, they have a function of passing on different kinds of therapeutic structure and security, and as such they are no different than conventional therapists.

Furthermore, it can be deduced from the above patient transcripts that what is projected onto the therapists is often quite positive. Obviously, when patients experience considerably less reservation, they can "open" themselves up and extend their trust better to the therapists, probably due to a reduction in anxiety between people abetted by the entactogens. Because the therapeutic relationship is in its core aligned to recreate adequate interhuman trust, psycholytic group sessions may serve as catalysts for (re-) experiencing inter-human trust. Interestingly, as seen in the clinical testimonials here, these experiences do not lead to an idealization of the therapists which would hinder therapy, despite a certain intensification of positive transference.

Also stressed in the patient descriptions is how therapeutic the interventions were for difficult situations during the psycholytic process. The basic aspects of giving security, active listening, and physical attention (holding hands, stroking, quieting) can further individual therapeutic goals as well as prove critical for involvement in debate, gentle confrontation, giving support, or even simple reference to a person's limits or situation.

4. Degree of control over the drug experience

Tremendous attention can be devoted to the fear of losing control, of not being able to control one's inner awareness when it is intensified by entactogens.

As experiments by Leuner (1962) have already shown, when administered a correctly tailored dose, patients can be well positioned to controlling the essential parts of the inner flow of their experiences and reactions while also preserving coherent contact with their surroundings. This point is also relevant because of the danger of re-traumatization resulting from an overpowering experience. On the other hand, considerable therapeutic potential is concealed in the chance to be able to "surrender" to an "autonomously" running process. While stressful moments can occasionally appear, such excessive demands rarely occur.

This unique therapeutic potential with LSD and related compounds is especially valid with entactogens, which cause considerably less change in cognition and the ability to control (Hess 1997, Naranjo 1973).

> "I had the feeling I was able to steer and shape experiences. If, for example, a fire were to break out, I would stand up orderly, pack my things, go downstairs, and give any reporter a fully complete report on the outbreak of the fire without disrupting this inner openness in any way...I was able to shape things very consciously. I also never had the feeling that I was helplessly being pulled into a whirlpool. On the contrary, I could set a caesura and say, 'I will try to put that into words' (although that went without words). 'Stop, back again' (really like a video recorder)—pause, 'stop, carry on, back again,' like a picture on hold, which you can enlarge out; but in this case for feelings." (57)

> "You can steer a lot, but you cannot steer everything. If you try to force the steering, it becomes a mad fight all the time...with me it was fear, that was something new, the unknown rose up. When I was more ready to do this later, I did not steer it. Then came the issue, which was due to be dealt with, and I was able to accept it." (68)

> "At the beginning, you are inclined to let yourself be carried by the [drug's] effect. But with time you learn that you can go deeper into your thoughts; you try not to lose the thread. Always [you are] coming back to the subject in order to look in more detail and get to the bottom of things. That got more interesting with each journey and...I took it more and more seriously...concentrated more and more, to keep chasing things up, go in deeper, and to get more answers for myself." (37)

"In a wonderful way, everything is intertwined... You are in every single layer, mentally present. You can even stop the picture in the middle of it, almost as if I had a video recorder and were to look at it and say, 'Stop, go back over the scene. What does that mean?' or 'I'll make a note of that for later.' But, I can also quite simply give myself up to it with physical feelings." (52/53)

These descriptions show that the ability to control appears to be considerably preserved. To an extent, it is really possible to learn how to use the altered mode of awareness so that after a few sessions the experience appears to become easier to self-direct; for such individuals it is as if there are training wheels to keep one in balance and able to see a clear horizon ahead instead of wobbling and watching the ground below. However, some people cited the opposite. These individuals feel that the diminished capacity to direct the experience advances them into unknown areas of themselves or into new areas of experience not thought possible for oneself or even known. Of particular interest is the capacity for targeted access of particular memories, much like hypnotherapy without the induction of a formal trance. Such insights appear as if they were played from a video recorder in that they can be zoomed in on, specifically investigated, extended, and then put into a new context. At such moments, the patients feel empowered to go deeper into the facets of their life that create hardship and are emboldened to recast their self-assessment in a new light.

Psychotherapeutic experiences with entactogens

1. Elements of therapeutic processing

a. Decreased anxiety, enhanced opening up, and building of trust

Entactogens, such as MDMA and MDE, exercise their effects on the mind essentially through anxiety reduction, but not in the same fashion as anti-anxiety sedative hypnotics do. The neurobiological substrate of entactogens' psychopharmacology can begin to explain why these compounds offer a different access point for reductions in anxiety. Under MDMA, a significant reduction of metabolism in the brain's left amygdala is found (Gamma et al.), a region shown to be involved in maintaining the "fear network" of the brain (Bandelow 2001).

Examples of anti-anxiety are found in the following interview excerpts:

> "With MDMA, I am simply fully 'softened,' and that was quite important for me. It is as if all barriers have fallen, as if all emotions are simply allowed...a softened up situation, which opened me up. I did not have any control anymore over whether I open myself up or not. That was exactly the point that I am actually, or was, too much controlled. That disappeared. Then, I was already somehow, almost rather clinging, soft, open, and chatty; something I did not recognize [as me before]." (10)

> "It was first of all a perception in my whole body...also felt physically, that barriers in me really dissolved. And through these...—already almost vital, physical perceptions— [and] there then came secondarily the level which is also the...concrete experiences from childhood until now. After a first, light tenseness, I became very trusting...as if I had [been] led down in a fast river, in the knowledge, that I would be floating and not sink. [I] have experienced, quite physically, something like a primal sense of trust or confidence...a feeling, as if I were descending into the depths via a spiral staircase, but not in a dark, creepy cellar, but in lower levels, fully neutral. To experience a severing from bodily barriers, which was unbelievably fascinating, because I realized in that moment, how...tensed up I otherwise am in my everyday life..." (50/51)

"Under LSD, it was such that I asked myself a question at the beginning and...worked on this quite ambitiously. Then all feelings appeared, which had to do with it...Once on LSD, I was scared. This anxiety became ever bigger towards everything. In the end, I was scared of the wind, scared of the air, scared of everything. That was almost a wonderful feeling, living through this anxiety—because it went into such great detail. Once a fly flew past me, and I was even scared of that and at the same time I noticed: I am not scared really, but I am in some way scared. This anxiety reached into the microscopically small. Somehow I got used to this anxiety, and just as I had got used to it, it was gone. Then I suddenly missed it because I did not know what I should keep myself busy with, except for the anxiety...There I caught myself—so the realization that I was holding on to the anxiety in order to then also [avoid] doing nothing... And then it disappeared and since then I have also never had this feeling again." (11)

"Once I had built up such an intimacy that I felt so comfortable next to the therapists and had that feeling, he must now stay with me and I am talking with him and I would like best of all not to let him go because it is so cozy at the moment. It was such a feeling that I had, so very friendly, cozily intimate. But without any ambitions to go any further: [it had] more to do with friendship. That was a big step for me, to come so far, to be exposed to something so human-friendship-like." (16)

"The change in state after the taking the substance... It is as if the ribcage were to open, breathe in deeply and submerge, just gliding along with an enormous feeling of luck. If you have...experienced that once and it happens again, it is simply indescribable. So opening and well-being at the same time, bodily well-being, feeling good oneself and to creep under your blanket and to be wonderfully at ease with yourself. Yes, also sensual. One is very awake, very active, but I always felt kind of soft. I was very relaxed, very attentive, but relaxed." (36)

"MDMA is...the opening of the heart and opening of feelings. For me at the beginning there was very great anxiety because that was exactly my difficulty—not to allow my feelings to run free. I tensed up. It was cold. I was scared, scared, scared. Just like it always was, that is, always when any feeling was about to show: I got scared. I also exactly saw or felt this defense mechanism, this fight when under MDE or MDMA. I can carry on, or I can slowly try to let myself enter into it in small steps and to let the feeling come, to feel, as in to feel my body. Then during the course of the sessions this also changed. More and more feeling came and I then felt more and more trust in myself...My heart opened even further, I also had the possibility to access all my emotions, to access pictures, also to access fears, to see them. I was also scared that the fears would disappear, that they were not fears at all, and I had made my own panic myself." (62)

"Now I'll briefly come to the L [LSD]. That was more comfortable for me because I could be a bit more controlled, as in I was more present in my head, I was clearer, I could structure myself better. I also felt my emotions but in a different way, meaning my head was able to deal with it better ...I was more creative under LSD. I experienced colors differently and music differently, I didn't have this stiffness in my body anymore...I was more relaxed under L. For me it was important that I [was able to] bring my head and emotion into good contact with one another." (62)

"The central, changing element in these experiences...is difficult to describe. It has many layers. There were inner events there, which played out on a lot of levels...The most central is definitely...that everything (which seemed to me to be problematic, impossible to solve, or denied) made sense in a quite peculiar, unified way. Without distinguishing between spirit, body, and soul. These three levels came together with each other in unison and suddenly appeared to pull together on one string; when it came to ideas, when it came to experience, also when it came to the 'looking the truth in the eyes'... This unity of otherwise always separately functioning layers was very meaningful...[where] before compromises were always made. What else is there to be done with three siblings who have badly fallen out, who now somehow have to keep a bit quiet? Suddenly the three were united and all agreed...[with] suddenly the feeling, we are now a force, together we are much better." (54)

These descriptions illustrate that, under the effect of entactogens, the basic balance between fear and trust is altered with an increased profound trust in oneself, one's own energies, and the goodwill and "goodness" of others. This reduction in anxiety goes hand in hand with the possibility of an extended self-exploration of motive, background, emotional state, and events in one's own biography. Due to the altered framework of consciousness, the usual channels in which associations move are also changed and a "new contextualizing" of past experience can occur (similar to "reframing" in hypnotherapy). Remarkable is the original and nevertheless meaningful logic in this relocating of experiences, people, and events. Because cognitive abilities are only slightly impaired under the effect of entactogens (Passie et al. 2005a), it is possible to quite freely connect those aspects of the experience that activate or further open up emotions while preserving cognitive functions and reasoning.

This "reorganization" is a desirable element of entactogen-assisted therapy and can go very deep and have lasting effects.

Because personal idiosyncrasies and the backgrounds of others are perceived with enhanced empathy and acceptance, a treatment that creates conditions for a period of re-evaluation of values (such as kindness, patience, acceptance, compassion, grace,) can also lead to lasting changes in relationships.

b. Psychophysical relaxation and altered perception of one's body

Entactogen responders report feeling fundamental psychophysical relaxation. The body is perceived as very pleasant and free from tension. Through deep-reaching psychophysical relaxation, many feel a deep sense of security conveyed by the whole body (Adamson and Metzner 1988).

> "It was first of all a perception in my whole body...[that was] also felt physically, that barriers in me really dissolved. And through these...already almost vital, physical perceptions, there   secondarily came the level of the...concrete experiences from childhood until now. After a first, light tenseness, I became very trusting...as if I had been led down in a fast river with the knowledge that I would be floating and not sink. [I] have experienced, quite physically, something like a primal sense of trust or confidence: ...a feeling, as if I were descending into the depths via a spiral staircase, but not in a dark, creepy cellar, but rather in lower levels, fully neutral. To experience a severing from bodily barriers, which was unbelievably fascinating, because I realized in that moment how...tensed up I otherwise am in my everyday life..." (50/51)

A pronounced need to be close and the reduction of inner barriers towards physical approaches and bodily contact can lead to completely new experiences in interconnectedness with other people. Shame and the feeling of endangering emotional integrity, which are usually of a determining nature, are less rigid under these conditions with entactogens.

It is important to recognize that these often very positively valued experiences of intimacy concern sexually neutral physical intimacy. Entactogens may stimulate a need to be near others but do not create any actual sexual stimulation (Zemishlany 2001, Buffum and Moser 1986). This is congruent with the extensive observations by Swiss therapists, who do not report a single case of eroticized behavior during psycholytic group sessions (Gasser 1996, Styk 1997). A plausible explanation for these "de-eroticized" opportunities for physical and human intimacy is given by Passie et al. (2005b), who offer a hypothesis of a psychophysiological equivalence between MDMA/MDE-induced conditions and the post-orgasmic condition.

For many, entactogen-assisted therapy offers enormous possibilities for exploring physical and human nearness free from sexual motives. Such therapy can create the opportunity to be open (once again) to positive experiences of intimacy and also to feel such emotions while feeling safe.

c. Acceleration of psychological processes

A prominent effect of entactogens is the ability to experience emotion promoted by the patient's latent psychodynamism. Common within the therapeutic framework is the confrontation with anxiety, sympathy, and love, as well as unappraised and problematic relationships. The reactivation of traumatic events of the past may also occur, but this usually happens in such a way as to make the emerging material accessible for those affected. Rather than directly activating an acute cycle of anxiety, the recollection of trauma can be self-evaluated within a profound inner calm. The construction of a more organized understanding of traumatic events becomes possible, which further aids in corrective processing. Things become clear in a very differentiated, emotional, and intellectual way, with the recollection and discovery of factual circumstances and relationships both present and past. Also common are patients finding a more global view of their inner psychological problems and connections as well as a therapeutic splitting of elements of their ego, each deconstructed for evaluation, reflection, and possible reformation.

> "Once I actually had a roundtable of my inner councils before my inner eye: reason, creativity, desire, and anger were sitting there and they were all allowed to give one comment. I had the impression my 'self' was present as adjudicator and said: 'so, we have a problem now, how can we solve it?' Each was allowed to make a contribution. Anger said, 'smash everything up.' Desire said, 'Come on, let's just do something else.' Reason said, 'Well, I don't expect that will end well.' All were allowed to listen and to say something. All sorts of ideas turned up. I listened to everything and then at the end decided, 'I think we will do it like this.'" (58)

Regression to an earlier time in life is also sometimes reported; it allows a very realistic reliving of past events. Also of interest is the occasional appearance of alternate simulations of formative situations from the past, encapsulated in an inner realm of experience. Despite the similarities in the flow of experience with dreaming, or daydreaming, with these out-of-the-ordinary and intensive forms of experiencing, no dreamlike fragmentation or alienating distortion of awareness occurs. Exaggerated forms of intrapsychological processes are found in compressed scenic-synoptic recapitulations of essential threads of formative biographical events. Also bound up with the described processes is the occurrence of the suspicion, feeling, and recognition of one's own possibilities and resources.

"One example of a concrete experience during the sessions was: I once had an abortion, and, under MDMA/MDE, I was able to take my leave from the child in a very nice manner. I saw the picture once again and was able to let go. I previously always had such a feeling of guilt in me, that it ought not to have happened and that I should not have had it done. That was very pleasant for me under MDMA/MDE because I once again could enter into this feeling of sadness...and then I also had the picture clear in front of me, this child, just as I had imagined it. And I found my peace through this because, through the opening of the heart, I was able to gently access this guilt once again." (63)

d. Regression

Regression is defined as a return to the psychological/mental structure or functions of an earlier stage of life. Occasionally, under the influence of an age-regressive process, different consecutive phases are re-experienced. Memories, at first mostly fragmentary and with unclear beginnings, may then take on an increasingly clearer form and, due to the intensity of their re-experiencing, transiently transform the individual to a past self.

Regression in the setting of psycholytic therapy was first investigated by Fernandez-Cerdeno (1964) and Zegans et al. (1967). In contrast to regression via hypnotic procedures (see Scott 1993), in psycholytic sessions it is more likely to occur spontaneously and be issue-orientated, with the associated reactivated experiences being very intense. Furthermore, psycholytic-induced regression is experienced with inner involvement of psychological conflicts of that past—as if quite realistically the person truly is of that age once more. This can be accompanied by a hypermnestic experiencing of inner scenes, senses, and sensations, as if a lifetime is peeled away revealing what was again as fresh and new: what "was" becomes once more as special as what "is." These intense experiences thus evoke strong emotions with affected abreactions.

"The memories were decisive because they were perceived as if I were [once again] a child and had a second chance again. So as if I could be such and such an age once again and was allowed to do everything one more time. What would I do differently? In this internal laboratory I was able to do this. I knew very well that this did not match with reality, but I suddenly discovered: There are ways to solve things, it occurred to me what to do. They were symbolic but actually forward-looking as well. I will do it in such and such a way when I am outside, when I am grown-up, and I am grown-up when the sitting is over. But not like a finished timetable...but an instinctive emotional knowledge with an optimism and a pleasure in doing it, like you only have when you are a child." (52/53)

"The painful experiences, they were kind of biographical. I knew exactly when this great pain came to be. For example I have always known
that, when I was four years old, my father went away for one year. He
had to go...and I relived this pain as a four year-old, and then I knew
this pain was so hefty from the perspective of a four year-old child. At
this moment, I understood that I had lived through the pain of loss and
that I had encapsulated this pain. I never felt it and never recognized
it. Only by means of such a journey was I able to come across it and
could explain to myself; why I had become so hardened at that moment.
Namely, because this pain, which I did go through, was so hefty. It must
really have bowled me over or threatened or destroyed me that my
father went away. I do not know how that worked, but, after I reexperienced this pain, the problem was solved. Since then, I do not feel any
diffuse melancholy anymore and also no fear of loss or anything sad. I
have often been confronted with pain which has then explained the rest
for me; why I am one way or another. And through the encounter with
this pain I then resolved the matter. Then it was gone..." (13)

Biographical events of great subjective importance drive regressions and form the
core of the entactogen experience. In his discussions on psycholytic therapy with the
entactogen methylendioxyamphetamine (MDA), Naranjo (1973) placed regression
as a reliable experience in psycholytic therapy and named its specifications as
follows: [During regression with MDA] "...the patient simultaneously regresses and
retains awareness of the present self. The person remembers more than conceptually,
as he may vividly recapture visual or other sensory impressions inaccessible to him
in the normal state, and he usually reacts with feelings that are in proportion to the
event. All the way from hypermnesia to repetition of a past experience in which not
only the old feelings are again felt" (Naranjo 1973: 26). In contrast to the regression
that may occur under LSD, under the effects of entactogens there is no LSD-typical
alteration of cognitive processes. As previously mentioned, it is an essential point
of therapeutic potential that entactogens do not lead to a regression of cognitive
functioning but to a memory-led age regression, in the sense of a differentiated re-
experiencing with a preserved ego structure and maintained abilities of cognition.

e. Rescripting of past behaviors or events
Entactogen-induced regression can engender creative and constructive processes.
Within the framework of therapeutic ego splitting (meaning one part of the self
regresses, while another part retains the perspective of present maturity), past
situations are not only reexperienced but also can be reappraised through newly
available creative powers that had been absent at that younger time.

It appears that, via this interplay of past and present, one can resolve the fixation on an outdated pattern, insofar as one is able to recognize possibilities for dealing with the past while it again feels "fresh."

"Exactly this mix, that you quite instinctively once felt, that things can also be done differently, and that you are not trapped in this childish problem-solving behavior (which you have become accustomed to almost like a spinal reflex and which you always thought you could not do differently). [For all] that you suddenly see: Of course it can be done differently. With absolute inner certainty [you can] say: Yes, that can be done differently; but of course it can be done different! That is not rubbish, ...no, that was a very practical, a very grown-up feeling, a joy in trying things out you believed would work. I always went out with this tool kit, and these changes also worked out really well for me...in the true sense of the meaning. And that was very lucky. Up until then I had always done everything that I thought I needed to change, like a well-behaved model pupil... But that something like this could also have anything to do with a sometimes cheeky, funny creativity, I would have never thought [possible]." (53)

"There was a situation having to do with my relationship with my clinging mother, and I said: She is always in my childhood bedroom, she never gets out of my life. Here I experienced it as a child, that she is always in my childhood bedroom...in the session. It does not matter what I do, she is always there; and then I called it out really loudly into the room: Get lost, get out, yes, get out of here! [I tried] a thousand possibilities, in an almost childlike desire to experiment: Which tone does she react to so that she finally gets out of here? Then I felt it consciously: I cannot manage it purely physically. I did feel quite small really, not hopelessly inferior, but I suddenly developed strategies [on] how I could get her out of there... Then I also screamed, swore, stomped on the floor with my foot...and then I suddenly started having creative ideas. What could you do with such an apparently unsolvable situation to finally make it disappear? This with an almost childlike curiosity and then quite simply—that it was also a wonderfully simple solution—to say: OK, I'll leave then. Yes. And, then, in this picture inside me, I left; she can stay in my childhood room then. Have fun!" (52/53)

Important for discovering alternative strategies for dealing with such situations is, of course, an explanation of that which had happened or had been experienced in the past. This entering into the past (which is common also in psycholytic therapy) with a reflecting ego remnant preserved hand-in-hand with an expanded perspective, contributes to a clarifying reordering of the past.

"[I had always] pictured abuse which had happened [to me]. That disappeared quite well under MDMA/MDE. Importantly, I found this feeling towards my father again; felt this love once again, which he had given me at that time. In the beginning, this was more of a black and white picture. But over the course of time this changed, so that in the end under MDMA or MDE, I was able to say: I can perceive this feeling towards him... I saw him as a picture, saw him as a father with this feeling in addition. It was a different, dancing feeling. There was simply a beautiful resonance between us when I was a child. In addition, I noticed that this abuse had never happened, that it was my mind, that it was me, who had thought it up. It was a small defiant child's act of revenge; I was very disappointed that my parents had split up... Because of this, I also felt this nagging fear, which I then had later towards other people, other men, that they might disappoint me again. It became clear to me that I had decided as a young child: I would never again get involved with any people who tell me that they love me. I simply did not want anything to do with that again. I then also saw this in pictures: this child, which had resisted, and [I] said, 'No, I don't want to.' I also noticed how I ruin things for myself with this..." (63)

"On LSD I then learned how I can deal with the disappointed child, how I find out for myself what is good for me or how I can find trust in myself, in order to take this disappointed child in my arms again and say: Let's go now, now we will grow up a bit and we will take this road together." (63)

"[I have profited] the most through the inner experiences, through the pictures, in the way in which I saw myself confronted with my questions... Yes, it sometimes seemed to me to be like running around a cul-de-sac for decades long, without noticing that it is one. And suddenly to see that there are endless possibilities within the cul-de-sac to develop something else; if it is one at all or, rather, that it isn't one. And at which point in my life I have to stop in order to say, 'Right, left, straight ahead, or if it went into a cul-de-sac: Stop, we'll go back [to] that symbol for my future life, bringing up the experiences again, which led me to becoming blind." (48)

Psycholytic processes, such as those described above, can be classified as belonging to the clarification processes relevant to psychotherapy, according to the prominent Swiss psychotherapy researcher Grawe (1995) (Schlichting 2000).

f. Problem actualization and corrective new experiences

Grawe (1995) understands "problem actualization" to mean that which has to be changed—according to the "principle of real experience"—in therapy or under therapeutic conditions and which can also be experienced in reality. Apart from updating the problem, corrective new experiences also play an important role in the processes of change.

"Once I had an experience of trust. You see, during this session I had absolutely no trust in the surroundings, the therapists, the people there, and it was all completely awful for me. I then gained awareness of trust through conversations with the therapists. I learned what it feels like to trust in the situation. I never trusted other people before (well, I did—as long as I had everything under [my] control). But to simply put myself in a situation and trust another person, that he helps me and is good to me: I have never known that. I was confronted with this situation in the sessions—this side of me, my mistrust, and then the feeling of really experiencing trust. Since having this session, I can trust—not continuously, not always, but through the experience of trust, trust was awakened in me. And that has also never left me again..." (14)

"In my world of feelings, it was like this, that I once again relived precisely these points, or rather these situations on my [therapy-] journey, which had hurt me in the course of my life. I then often experienced it differently than how I still remembered it—how it had been, or how it was in my world of feelings. For instance, when my parents' separated: I had the feeling that my father had never loved me because he left us. On a [therapy-] journey, I then once again became aware of my parents separation, but above all I recognized that they had not separated because of me. This took away my feeling of guilt. Before this, I had always had the feeling that it was my fault that they had separated. I saw on this journey that it was actually many disputes that had been involved but that I had nothing to do with it. I even realized that their love for me had not lessened. Before, I always had the feeling that they then did not love me anymore because of what happened." (66)

"There was a meeting with a man at a session, where I found the courage to approach the male part. Initially this fear was naturally there: Should I let myself get involved or should I not? Ultimately it was a wonderful experience. I could get involved with this male participant. For the first time, I lost this fear of closeness, which had always been a real issue for me...I trusted my feelings and was able to get involved and this was also accepted. That was the most important thing for me because it meant I could trust my feelings. It was very important for me that I had also gotten to know this male side in a very different way. Before, I had always been very mistrustful and saw men in a very poor light. And then suddenly I had a very different encounter..." (67)

These quotations demonstrate how neurotically constricting experience and behavioral patterns, which account for prominent parts of the patient's suffering, can become accessible for new interpretation and processing when they are brought to life within the framework of psychotherapeutic processes. In this context, not only concrete experience of constrictive patterns, but also their alteration through new experiences (with other content and outcome) are decisive. According to Grawe, it is essential "...that the patient actually experiences what this is all about..." (Grawe 1995: 137). This "actual experiencing" can be extremely condensed with reduced anxiety and increased openness to new experiences that is characteristic of psycholytic therapy. Far-reaching effects of trust building and interhuman relationships will unfold.

g. Transpersonal experiences

From the earliest clinical experiences with hallucinogens onward, it is well known that many people have mystical experiences gaining insight into archetypal higher contexts, or problems of humanity, in an unusual way (Grof 1975, Masters & Houston 1966). Mystical experiences can have strong triggering effects on psychotherapeutic development with resultant distinct effects on a person's orientation in life and worldly values (empirically proved by Griffiths et al. 2006, McGothlin et al. 1967, Pahnke 1962).

In sessions with psycholytic doses, such experiences are not particularly frequent (compared to the psychedelic approach using much higher doses, Grof 1980), but they do regularly occur. Since they are nearly unknown in the framework of virtually all other psychotherapeutic procedures, they constitute a specific feature of psycholytic therapy.

"The first trips always tended to have something rather negative; no, in retrospect something super positive, but, in that moment, negative because I was confronted by some other side in me, or by a situation which was painful, stressful, or sad. Later, I had the impression as if knowledge was welling up from within me, and that was very exhilarating. I had the secure feeling that I had understood a lot about the interrelationships of the world. Suddenly I knew what love really is...as if I had read a clever book, but I then also felt it. Yes, those are interrelationships that I then understood. The universe, life, death, war, freedom: such fundamental issues that I suddenly understood or could feel. The wonderful thing was that I knew what it is, what love or freedom is. But I couldn't formulate it, and that was exactly what the sublime experience was. It could not be put into words and nevertheless it was very clearly there, could be felt, and was visible. Those were wonderful episodes. This occurred for the first time in the last sessions, as...my concerns were no longer so much in the foreground, I mean, only after the clutter had been removed." (12/13)

"In the first session, where I had this bodily release and redemption, I also felt a love of myself in a way that I had never experienced before. You can certainly also see this as a sort of spiritual experience. It was so close to the heart and close to my feelings and with a certainty which could be physically felt; the knowledge that I am carried by some type of love which is in me and flows through me if I open myself up... But, precisely, the love is within me, so that the questions of whether my parents also really loved me as dearly as I always wanted them to, and what were all the things they did so wrong, suddenly became so unbelievably boring. That meant that this catalog of sins, which I have searched through as meticulously as a tax inspector, was no longer exciting." (53/54)

"When I was on MDMA or MDE, I had the feeling that I melted into myself, into nothingness or into another form of life, or that I was simply somewhere; I had the feeling that I was simply in a sort of world of colors. It was wonderful and it was beautiful and I was simply nothing. That was a wonderful occurrence, a very beautiful feeling, to simply be nothing." (52/53)

"These sessions trigger things, ...that slumber deep inside you, which are otherwise hidden...It touches my very innermost being...The beautiful thing about one of these sessions was that afterwards I felt a complete sense of well-being. The effect lingers on to this very day. To have had this experience, has nothing to do with prestige, money, or anything else. That—for me at least—is the meaning of life: to be, simply just to be." (24)

"The first journey was simply marvelous, and I believe I thanked the therapist a hundred thousand times because this experience was of inestimable value. What I felt about myself, how I felt about myself, to be so close to myself, to be able to open up myself like this, to be able to talk about myself." (37)

"After I had the second journey, I called it 'sobering' because it was really the opposite of the first one. It seemed that the first journey had given me a basis which had strengthened me. I felt at ease with myself... but the second journey was exactly the opposite. It became very critical. There I saw the loss of my child, and I experienced this as the loss of part of me as a person. I also tried to look into this, to see why this happened, and where this child is now. That also meant saying farewell. That was very tough." (37)

"But on all journeys, even though there were tough moments, the feeling of happiness actually always dominated, and after a while there were always very long moments of relaxation, the feeling of happiness, bliss, joy, and participation in everything which was around me." (37)

For LSD, the occurrence of "peak experiences" (Maslow) or "integral experiences" (Masters & Houston 1966) has been described to occur at the drug's early stage effects. During this, the person experiences a type of subjective "ascent" into a new level of awareness with intense moments that are often overwhelming. The emotional charge is powerful, even if the experience outwardly appears calm. The person in question intensely perceives how to move within the deepest levels of human awareness, understood as an essence, existential source of life, or God. Sense of ego instead is felt more as an illusion, loses its shape, and appears to dissolve into a larger, more comprehensive being. Sherwood et al. (1963) were the first to describe the personality-altering effects of such "psychedelic experiences." Pahnke and Richards (1966) systematically examined the phenomenology of psychedelic-induced mystical experiences and their implications. They stress the identical nature of these experiences with those of religious mystics and also emphasize their personality-altering effects within the framework of psychotherapeutic processes.

For the material discussed here, it must be stressed that the vast majority of the experiences described by the participants were while under the influence of entactogens. Peak experiences also occurred, which, however, typically take on another form. As the descriptions show, these appear to center on an affirmation of the individual aspects of the self, while in the case of LSD it is rather the dissolution of the ego and an encounter with a comprehensive transcendence common to LSD. In contrast, the loss of ego under entactogens tends to be described as dissolution of the constriction imposed on the ego through previous life events. This loosening of the usually "hard boundaries" of the ego is characterized by an openness toward the subjective world achieved through (self) acceptance. Worldly things and interrelations by no means disappear in the face of a superordinated transcendent. Instead, perceptions are changed by fear reduction and peace of mind resulting in a strengthened impression of basal intactness and orderliness in (the person's own) life. One gains possession of a sense that nothing else is required to be happy because everything is available in the self-abandonment to a deep peace.

Naranjo (1973), who gathered experiences in psychotherapy with both hallucinogens and entactogens, describes the peak experiences under hallucinogens with the term "depersonalization" and those under entactogens as "personalization."

The characteristic elements of transpersonal experience, described above, are as follows:

1. A completely relaxed opening up toward the inner awareness.
2. Feeling free/permitted for self-love; an ability to accept oneself with basal self-acceptance.
3. Feeling an emotional, relaxed detachment to an extent that everything appears as being in order and safe.
4. A positively felt convergence with an inner core.
5. A recognition and feeling of what love is.
6. A conscious awareness of non-material aspects of being and happiness.

2. Integration and therapeutic changes

a. The process of integration
In contrast to sessions with entactogens or hallucinogens that are not supervised by a therapist, the integration of experiences into everyday life can actively be worked on in drug-assisted psychotherapy. Such work for integration may be particularly necessary for two reasons:

1. The altered framework of consciousness intensifies awareness, further activates unconscious material, intensifies the provision of new insights, and leads to a loosening of ego structure. The strangeness of some experiences in the altered state of awareness as well as a possible increase in permeability of the unconscious to consciousness, turn the integration of these experiences into a therapeutic task.

2. The insights gained during psycholytic sessions can only be suppressed with great difficulty because they were derived within the framework of the patient's own psychological processes—with only limited participation by the therapists. In some cases, patients were able to destabilize established intrapsychological narcissistic balances.

Even if this emotional destabilization can sometimes be problematic, it is generally beneficial for processes of change, since mental processes become more receptive to new experiences and influences. It can also condition familiar behavioral patterns to become more flexible. But even with this loosening up and destabilization, the psycholytic work does not have to lead to an overburdening, since—as the many years of with psycholytic therapy would suggest (Leuner 1981) —they are subject to autoregulative mechanisms, which only allow as much material as can be processed.

> "Actually I never had the feeling of being overburdened by an episode or of not being able to integrate it. Well, you can only experience as much as you can bear, you can process, [or] as much as you can take in. Once, I had a very intensive session, and on Sunday evening I became increasingly depressed and practically couldn't sleep that night. I just cried and wrote. On Monday, I couldn't go to work and continued to cry and write. On Tuesday, it was over, and I could carry on again just as normal...I can tell you, because it was only my second journey, I was afraid that things would get out of control, and that I had participated in something that I no longer had under control. But it turned out that the opposite was the case: you know I was able to write an incredible amount, to write a great deal about how little I was loved, [and] how much I had been left in the lurch. I was also able to put the blame on my father and mother. At one time it was enough and over and done with. Then I went to work completely as normal and was not overburdened at all. That naturally gave me trust for the next journeys. And then, I always knew: I don't need to be afraid at all..." (46)

People frequently describe a phase of turbulence immediately after their psycholytic sessions or during the following days. Even if no such turbulence manifests, an inner fermentation of that which was experienced occurs, taking the patients further. Here, not only conscious but also unconscious assimilation processes probably play a role (Grof 1980). After a few days from the session, important parts of integration have already taken place, and the newly won insights can be integrated into everyday life. Also, everyday life provides opportunities to reflect on the insights and experiences won during the psycholytic sessions and/or to incorporate them into practice.

> "I had to spontaneously cry and didn't know why...there was somehow a mourning process which I only understood much later. The relation-ships between things fell into place...always a few days or months lat-er...Towards the end of the sessions I always had emotional outbreaks; I was so shaken up by the whole process then, by what I had seen there. At the end, shortly before or while the effect wore off...I was often very shaken up inside and weepy and had fits of sentimentality." (12)

> "At every session I participated in, there were things there which I was able to draw on afterwards...although I had not yet understood them

on the journey. Sometimes images just appeared or a feeling welled up without me being able to relate to them for the time being. But when the sessions were over one, two, or three days later, I was able to piece together the building blocks. In retrospect, I can say that every journey I made was a building block. I was able to put these building blocks together after a few sessions, and it provided an absolute meaning for me. There were also concrete things that I was able to change because of this..." (65)

"The wonderful thing is that afterwards (although this episode has a dimension that you are not familiar with in everyday life), when the journey is over, you can once again return to normal and good social interactions. It is not exalted and hysterical; instead you quite normally return to regular social interactions. The therapist remains the therapist and you don't now think: Ah my best friend, my father or something [about the therapist]... The therapist was once again just the therapist, but it was the contact, this depth, this ability to talk about yourself and to simply feel accepted, that was unique." (38)

Starting with dimensions of experience, many patients describe their individual psychodynamic psychotherapy sessions between their psycholytic sessions as very helpful for the task of integration.

"The processing of these experiences and their integration into everyday life were achieved, among other things, through the individual sessions. In these...sittings...I always summarized the whole. After the first journey I meditated every day for half an hour, in order to come to terms with it all...what I had experienced there, recapitulating again in a very disciplined way, every single day. I also wanted to really evaluate and integrate what I had seen and experienced there. Later I did not need to anymore. Since then I have the feeling that this happens on a daily basis, with every acquaintance I make, with certain feelings I experience; I always reflect upon what I experienced on the journey. Then I also suddenly recognize something again or discover something...I have changed and hence naturally also changed my environment. I have certainly confused some people because I have changed... In any case, all relationships, all encounters are more positive, purer, and clearer..." (18)

It also appears to be important that the patients devote some time to themselves, during the days after the psycholytic sessions, to allow the experiences to linger on, to process them, and put them into practice in everyday life.

"In order to process these experiences and integrate them into everyday life, I need plenty of peace and quiet for myself afterwards, with no distraction. I was very careful to make sure of this. So that this really consolidated once again...After a session I was once completely beside myself, I kept bursting into tears, couldn't sleep, and also had to directly consult with my therapist afterwards. I became aware of feelings of guilt which I couldn't cope with... I was then able to talk to him about this and then simply let these fits of tears take their course...After all, they belonged to the process. I also wrote everything down. That is another form of processing. Once a week I had a therapy session, where I brought up the subject of the perceptions I had gained in the sessions, including the images, the emotional outbreaks..." (31)

Many patients need to devote some time to themselves alone after their psycholytic sessions in order to process their experiences. Written records can advance understanding and integration of these insights. Systemic processes are also interesting, in how they come into being through changes of perspective and increased self-acceptance. As the example above illustrates, these insights may develop their own dynamism, which can considerably accelerate the processes of change through the environment of interpersonal connections.

"Relativizing my criteria takes place mostly in my head...That I have gotten to know a new friend, that I have simply accepted if he says to me, 'I find this and that really great about you.' That I then say to myself, 'Yes, that's right. He finds that great and doesn't put that into a question [about me] anymore'...At that moment when I receive a compliment to say to myself, 'Yes, you'll accept that now, it's right. Don't start to say, "Oh no, oh come on, it isn't really true"'...At such moments to say [instead], 'No, you keep your mouth shut now, don't relativize it.' [Replace those thoughts with] 'great, thanks, nice, I think that's good.' Also, it was very important that I could very clearly and in a friendly way show and say to my colleagues at work, 'The way you work is helpful to me, you have really taught me something, the way you do this and that and manage things, that was really instructive for me.' And the relationships [since doing so] became really great...And, well, that was simply a more honest, loving self-appraisal that I learned for myself and which helped me find my place, to simply feel at ease for where I am." (45)

b. Therapeutic results from the patient's perspective

Because the psychology diploma thesis upon which this work is partially based (interviews with patients) did not apply objective measures regarding therapy outcome, some relevant passages from patient interviews are to be considered single reports. These reports provide a description of the processes and results of change for this entactogen-assisted therapy, as presented from the patients' perspective.

"The psycholytic psychotherapy sessions gave me the courage to reorganize my life...The biggest step I took was in separating from my husband and daring to take a different path. This means that I take better care of myself and feel responsible for myself. Before, I felt too responsible for other people, and was fixated on others. The treatment sessions made it very clear to me that due to this I was not at all able to be at one with myself and that I had forgotten my sense of who I am...I saw the need, and I was able to find the strength to realize that if I am going to get better again, [then] I have to take action. And then I managed it, too. Okay, I still need support, but these weekends were actually the key to that...with an unbelievable permanence...When I read through my reports again, I am amazed at how they are all connected. There is a real common thread." (22/23)

"What these sessions changed for me was that perception became more intense and my relationships with people became clearer...Basically, I have a significantly deeper and better relationship with people. I can feel them more strongly and am more aware of them and respond to them better. I am much more empathetic now. Which of course means that some relationships that did not work after this have fallen by the wayside. Some people who saw how I changed could not deal with it." (9)

"Afterwards I did a lot of things; I simply did them. I felt an almost indescribable confidence in my own inner strength and ability. Whatever consequences, conflicts, or problems arose, [I felt] able to solve them. A feeling of total confidence that I did not know before because I was still making cautious, considered attempts which were still in need of a certain safeguard. I developed a much more direct contact with my deepest feelings. I think that it was from then on that I first began to feel what love is. My children are perhaps an exception. With them I have already felt profound love, which is what pushed me into therapy back then because I had already felt this at some point and realized that it did not otherwise exist in my life. Enthusiasm and courage, also at work, to develop things and not just to have them in the back of my mind, but to live them too... that is what has happened with my work and with my friends... There were of course painful changes, too—rifts, breaks—but I was suddenly much, much freer from fear and had a lot more courage." (50)

"I have a different access to my inner world, my emotional life. I am more at one with myself. I can better take myself to task. I am no longer afraid of my emotions. After the sessions I was prepared to enter into a new partnership, to be totally open for one. Actually it's thanks to these therapy sessions that I lost that fear, fear of myself and fear of my feelings." (61)

"The sessions gave me another type of self-confidence. I believe more in myself and thus developed a different kind of strength; I can follow my goals better and formulate what I want, which I couldn't do before. I was then able to begin to articulate my wishes and act on them, to set goals for myself and work on these goals...I came away from the sessions with a different strength and felt that I can have confidence in myself. So taking this, I went out into life and have begun to change things, step by step. This new, basic feeling, this love for myself: that is the strength that came out during these weekends. After the 'journeys,' I went to the individual therapy sessions and could discuss them with the therapist. I also got a lot out of that for myself." (69)

"The experiences that I had, the way I saw myself, got to know myself: they remain with me. I am now more aware of my tougher sides and also my loving sides. I see this in my work, too—I am less complicated, more natural and more approachable than before, and less under check. I don't have to prove so much. I am simply there and know that I may have things to do, but I just do them. The way you deal with people seems to be at least as important as the result of the task at hand. The experiences with the medicine helped a lot in dealing with people." (35/36)

A common feature of all these reports is the substantial increase in the patients' self-awareness. Patients become better at experiencing and understanding their own limitations and potential, and they develop greater self-acceptance. Additionally, there are increases in the sense of trust in oneself as well as in others, in emotions in general, and in changed interpersonal experiences. In terms of the categories by Grawe (1995), the effect called "changed meanings," in which the patient experiences himself and his environment, appears abundantly clear. As a result of these processes, there is a "mobilization of individual resources," which also aligns well to the perspectives of explanation according to Grawe (1995).

c. Comparisons with conventional psychotherapy
It is not hard to imagine that the intense and new experiences that occur in psycholytic sessions have distinctly different elements than conventional psychotherapy. Yet a special role is also played by the intensification of transmission of emotions (including anxiety reduction) and relevant content, especially in the increase of confidence and reduction of shame and fears of losing ones integrity.

"In contrast to conventional therapy, all bonds are broken. You have really deep, really open access to yourself. Truthfulness and really intense feelings and emotions [are experienced] that one otherwise rarely allows. Yes, just to be as you are, to let go of all facades and anxiety and to be able to be totally authentic, honest, and lovingly critical with yourself...To experience feelings...potentiated, as far as...what it means just to feel love inside yourself, for everything, not for one person or a few people...This happens only in such sessions...A therapy session otherwise only lasts one hour, while there you are in contact with all people...If a person usually has a problem opening up...this limitation doesn't exist on the journeys. That is why I said...you don't have a wall around yourself anymore. But it is not that you take it down, it just isn't there..." (46)

"The relationship to the therapist at the sessions was a very important factor because I saw him differently than in the normal therapy session. This was important for me because I had more trust...I could open up to him; I lost some of my anxiety and could tackle my problems better. He helped me do this, that is, he talked with me...I had the feeling that I could enter into discussion with him in a different way than in the normal therapy session and on a much deeper level." (67)

"What happens in normal sessions is what makes one able to function in society, maybe trying to put sticky plaster on the surface here and there and maybe it even helps. But my inner self was first reached through this other form of therapy, really reached and really changed. Not changed in the sense that I became another person but that I became free from all these crusts and residues, this hardening and walls. These are of course more quickly broken through with the drugs. In normal therapy, you can still protect and defend yourself through talking: you have a clear head and are in control. Yet through this loss of control, which happens because of the drugs, you are still reachable, and way down deep. You can also work your way down into your core self...Deep traumatic experiences, or deep residue and hardening, are reached with the use of these drugs, the intensity of the perception and...this form of work." (20)

"In regard to the difference between normal sessions and the psycholytic sessions...they are much more intense and go much deeper. You can, if you are prepared to, pull a lot more out of yourself. You can look at a lot more issues in a short time. You are more relaxed...than if you go to a therapist, where I go for maybe an hour between my work...For me, a weekend is more relaxed because you can concentrate on the issues you want to address beforehand. You can...go on the weekend trip with more structure. You have a lot more time; if you want you can spend 48 hours non-stop in your inner world. With a therapist, I go in for 45 minutes and talk about whatever is current...It is a lot more superficial, though I used the sessions to discuss the trips afterwards. This combination was very important to me." (70)

As already mentioned in the previous quotation, the therapeutic effect (including the group experience) extends over a period of about 48 hours, which can be an important opportunity for advancing the goals of the therapy. But the group experience, often deeply moving, ought to be seen as especially beneficial because, along with reduced anxiety, patients also came in contact with fundamental interpersonal and physical closeness in the therapy group. These are characterized by "spontaneous"—that is, independent of the patients—feelings of closeness and contact as an expression of the need for human closeness and physical contact. Patients can act on this need due to reduced anxiety (even patients with difficult past histories) without feeling that their own integrity is at risk. Closeness and contact occur without any sexual desire or ulterior motive. A sense of "hanging onto others" or the experiences made with them, rarely occurs beyond the session. Passie et al. (2005b) proposed a psychophysiological hypothesis to explain this phenomenon, suggesting that there is a parallel between entactogen-induced psychophysical states and the post-orgasmic state. This implies that, under the effects of entactogens, one is in a similar state of equivalent relaxation and sexual satiation as directly as after orgasm, and, as such, new possibilities may open up for integrating into therapy experiences obtained from non-anxious, nonsexual body contact.

What is very impressive and different from conventional psychotherapeutic processes are the intense regressions, interspersed with hypermnesia, often occurring as a conscious return to past experiences. A current, painful pattern serves as a bridge to the past. In these "regressions in the service of the ego" (Kris 1974), dissociations are not desired, which generally occur without a therapeutic ego-split and with the knowledge of the adult-ego. Rather, contact with reality and the therapist remain fully preserved. Important requirements for healing past wounds include a sense of safety and security, as well as centering oneself before entering the drug-supported trance. Requirements are ensured by the therapeutic framework and the therapeutic relationship. Regression, in the framework of a psycholytic session, is active, conscious, and not out of necessity, which underlies most other dissociative phenomena. A person wants to go there in order to overcome something, solve it in a different way, or correct it. Another difference from conventional therapy can be seen therein: that it is not primarily the therapist who suggests a solution here but the patient who independently brings it about in his or her inner world of experience.

Entactogens and psychotherapy

The psycholytic method is not an autonomous therapy. It is much more a tool that helps psychotherapy as routinely practiced and is rooted within psychoanalysis and psychodynamic psychotherapy.

Throughout the psycholytic sessions, a regular network of connotations and insights into the unconscious psychodynamics of the person appear more obvious (defense mechanisms of the ego, affective impulses, dream symbolism) to the carefully observing, supportive psychotherapist. These treatments have a special role in the overall therapy: in the decision to take this option, the sessions in preparation, the special responsibilities and transferences created during psycholytic sessions, and the post-psycholytic sessions that follow. In order for therapists to have useful preconceptions to observe and prepare for, the relevant effects and therapeutic implications of psychotherapy under the influence of entactogens is presented.

1. The entactogens MDMA and MDE

The major psychoactive substances used within psycholytic therapy are entactogens (MDMA, MDE, MDA) and some hallucinogens (psilocybin, LSD). Healthy people with eyes closed experience clear consciousness, intensified affectivity, and a dreamlike state with unfolding fantasies and thoughts, usually accompanied by intact self-perception and reality checking. Appropriate memory during the state is retained. Perceptual senses are altered or heightened, which may lead to visions, illusions and pseudo-hallucinations. Abstract thinking withdraws. Ideas and strings of thought appear coherently joined in meaning (and obey the rules of Freudian primary process). Pictorial, associative thinking engender emotional insight and manifest unconscious psychological content. Often the patient succeeds in synthesizing disparate, innermost psychological facts into a cohesive understanding, as if it is being seen from the perspective of an observer holding a camera with a wide-angle lens. Memories, relationships, experienced feelings, or faulty character traits come together into a new context that had not previously been identified as interrelated. While within the experience, various areas of consciousness are simultaneously accessed, so that a broad integration of unconscious material is able to occur. With intention and supportive guidance, the patient experiences an abundance of insights into neurotic attitudes. The nature of these insights usually harmonizes with the pronounced emotional involvement experienced through the session, and this, in turn, considerably deepens and accelerates the therapeutic process (Leuner 1981, Grof 1980). Insight into the therapeutic character of the situation is usually available ("reflecting remnant of ego," according to Leuner 1962). This ego residue will always be there with carefully selected individual dosage.

MDMA and MDE have a specific pattern of effects that can be assigned completely to neither the hallucinogens nor the stimulants (amphetamines). In fact, entactogens share certain characteristics with both of these groups. However, the main focal point of their effect lies in the area of emotion (Gouzoulis-Mayfrank et al. 1996).

Altered perception of time	90%
Increased ability to interact with or be open with others	85%
Decreased defensiveness	80%
Decreased anxiety	65%
Decreased sense of separation or alienation from others	60%
Changes in visual perception	55%
Increased awareness of emotions	50%
Decreased Aggression	50%
Aware of previously unconscious memories	40%
Decreased compulsiveness	40%
Decreased restlessness	30%

Table 2: Subjective effects of MDMA (from Liester et al. 1992)

In his first evaluation of the pharmacological specifics of entactogens, the medicinal chemist David Nichols, M.D., derived the term "entactogens" in the following way:

> "It seemed that the effect of these drugs was to enable the therapist—or patient—to reach inside and deal with painful emotional issues that are not ordinarily accessible. Just as the word "tact" has the connotation of communicating information in a sensitive and careful way so as to avoid offense, it seemed that the Latin root of this word, tactus, would be appropriate as part of the term. Addition of the Greek roots "en" (within or inside) and "gen" (to produce) created the term "entactogen," having the connotation of producing a touching within. This designation seems to have appropriate roots, is aesthetically pleasing to those who have heard it, and most importantly, appears to have no negative connotations for a potential patient." (Nichols 1986, p. 308)

In an appropriate environment, entactogens are expected to induce an easily controllable change in consciousness (especially with regard to how emotion impacts awareness), decreased anxiety, and pronounced psychophysical relaxation. Additionally, entactogens increase introspection and willingness to communicate. Attention can easily be directed towards emotionally meaningful issues. New aspects of one's own self, or one's own story, can be recognized and placed into a new context of meaning through an inner dialogue, made possible by anxiety-reducing effects ("the resolution of neurotic fear") that favor expansion of associative capacity. The overall catalytic effects push latent, otherwise unconscious inner systems of tension forward ("transphenomenal dynamic control systems" of Leuner 1962, "systems of condensed experience" of Grof 1975) to be resolved. The psychological content in these memory systems becomes conscious and made available for therapeutic processing.

Often these feelings and insights are accepted as "breakthroughs" that in turn enhance self-assurance, self-acceptance, and the empathic perception of others. In distinction to hallucinogens, cognitive functions and ego integrity remain largely unchanged by entactogens (Passie et al. 2005a). Intra-psychological defense mechanisms, though usually relaxed, continue to remain available to the ego. The entactogenic state merely offers the possibility, or rather the invitation, to "leave these mechanisms aside" and get to know oneself in a new way (Passie et al., 2005a, Hess 1997). A moderate adult dosage of MDMA or MDE lasts for four to six hours, but the relaxing effect on the body and psyche as well as the decreased anxiety may be perceivable during some additional hours.

2. Psychophysiological and neurobiological effects

Entactogens stimulate the sympathetic nervous system, the release of prolactin and cortisone, and cause a mild increase in blood pressure and heart rate (cf. Dumont and Verkes 2006, Passie et al. 2005a). Their psychological effects are only brokered secondarily via the dopamine system, primarily via a massive release and inhibition of the reabsorption of the neurotransmitter serotonin. Since all entactogens induce some degree of inhibition of the reuptake of noradrenalin (Vollenweider 2001), it also is possible that their psychoactive effects are due in part to this mechanism as well.

In a study on neurometabolism under the influence of the entactogen MDE (2 mg/kg p.o.) by means of [18F] FDG-positron emission tomography (PET) (Gouzoulis et al. 1999), no significant changes in global brain metabolism were found, but there was increased metabolism in the cerebellum and anterior cingulum and decreased cortical metabolism, particularly in the frontal regions. The FDG-PET study by Gamma et al. (2000) under MDMA (1,7 mg/kg p.o.) showed increases in the regional cerebral blood flow (rCBF) of the cerebellum, the ventral anterior cingulum, the ventromedial prefrontal cortex, the inferior temporal lobe, and the medial occipital lobe, possibly jointly caused by no irritation through an activation exercise during the experiment. Bilateral decreases could be seen in the pre- and para-central lobule, the dorsal and posterior cingulum, the superior temporal gyrus, the insular cortex, and the thalamus. Of particular significance is the deactivation of the left amygdala, a key structure of the brain's fear network which, as such, may be a key neurobiological substrate for the decrease in anxiety and induction of euphoria. The richly interconnected structures of the anterior and posterior cingulum, thalamus, temporal lobe, and cerebellum may form the central network in the regulation of mood and emotion (George et al. 1995).

An interesting fact is that the psychophysiological effects of entactogens promote a state similar to the one which usually occurs immediately after orgasm (post-orgasmic state) (Passie et al. 2005b) (Table 3). The left amygdala also becomes deactivated during the post-orgasmic condition (Komisaruk and Whipple 2005, Komisaruk 2008).

Psychophysiological functions	MDMA-induced condition	Post-orgasmic condition
General condition	deep relaxation	deep relaxation
CNS-arousal	increased	increased
Neurobiological	deactivation of the left amygdala	deactivation of the left amygdala
Cardiovascular prolactin increased	BP + pulse increased prolactin increased	Neuroendocrine
Vigilance	increased	increased (reduced)
Feelings	intensified	intensified
Anxiety	reduced	reduced
Thought	more imaginative	more imaginative
Experiencing sense of body	intensified	intensified
Mind set	opened	opened

Table 3: Psychophysiological similarities between a typical MDMA-induced condition and the post-orgasmic condition (modified from Passie et al. 2005b)

3. Neurobiological correlates specific to entactogens and psychotherapy

Recent neurobiological research shows that while under the influence of traumatic experience (that is, those that exceed psychological processing capacity), an abnormal processing of sensory stimuli occurs. Incoming sensory stimuli are normally distributed by the thalamus to various secondary brain structures for further processing. Before being incorporated into memory (via the hippocampus), sensory information is presorted within the amygdala according to its relevance in perceiving danger and survival. It is then fed into different parts of the cortex, further evaluated and categorized before being selectively stored in the memory system (Figure 1).

A "simplification" of processing occurs with traumatic experience (Figure 2). The processing is reduced to that which occurs in the phylogenetically older parts of the brain (the limbic system, amygdala, and hippocampus). In contrast, the more complex categorizing and evaluative processing via the cortex is "left out," and a kind of "immediate storing" of the unselected stimuli in the hippocampus occurs. In integration of later events, if sensory impressions arrive reminiscent of past trauma, then an over-activation of the amygdala occurs, without inhibition by means of the cingulum and the medial frontal cortex (Figure 3). In patients with posttraumatic stress disorder (PTSD), over-activation of the left amygdala is common (Liberzon and Sripada 2008) and correlates with clinical symptom severity (Shin et al. 2005). In contrast, the activity in the cingulum and the medial frontal cortex are strongly reduced (Nutt and Malizia 2004). There is a circuit between the amygdala and the ventromedial prefrontal cortex, which enables the latter to limit the amygdala's response. Indeed, under the influence of MDMA, activity decreases in the amygdala and increases in the prefrontal cortex (Gamma et al. 2000).

It appears possible that amygdala deactivation enhances access to memories recorded in the pathological mode described above. After experiencing trauma, the amygdala usually prevents a release of traumatic memories because such content is self-threatening, activating the brain's fear network (Figure 3). The benign amygdala deactivation suggests that otherwise inaccessible memories can be visited and become accessible for therapeutic reprocessing and integration. A rerun of traumatic events logged in memory opens an opportunity for revision "within the individual's capacity through trauma-therapeutic procedures" (Pagani et al. 2007). Such reprocessing of memory may be stored more appropriately in the memory system—this time including involvement of normative cortical pathways (Figure 4).

One could speculate that the combination of a deactivated amygdala and reciprocally activated cingular and prefrontal structures gives rise to a balanced reexperiencing of trauma-relevant memories during that state. Clinical evidence as well as our study suggest that during MDMA-assisted therapy, patients are virtually never without self-control nor feel they are in situations that otherwise might pathologically overwhelm them. Indeed, psychological awareness under the effects of MDMA leads "of its own accord" in the direction of a benign reprocessing of previous traumatic memories (Mithoefer et al. 2011, Mithoefer 2008).

There are more neurobiological mechanisms that contribute to the healing potential of MDMA or MDE (Figure 5). A major approach to treating PTSD is extinction learning in a therapeutic context. However, approximately 40% of patients continue to meet diagnostic criteria for PTSD with this method (Bradley et al. 2005). Combining this treatment with daily medications, such as SSRIs, has not shown much additive effect (Simon et al. 2008), and anxiety-reducing treatments may interfere with extinction learning (McNally 2007). In this regard, MDMA-assisted therapy offers a new option to enhance extinction learning and growth from new experiences because MDMA works on several neurobiological mechanisms involved in the pathophysiology of PTSD (Johansen and Krebs 2009). Clinical studies show that MDMA strengthens the therapeutic alliance, decreases avoidance behavior, and improves tolerance for reprocessing of painful memories (Mithoefer 2008, Greer and Tolbert 1986).

Another potential therapeutic mechanism of MDMA is its triggering of the secretion of the neurohormone oxytocin (Dumont et al. 2009). This hormone is involved in the encoding of positive social memories, particularly interpersonal trust and empathy (Guastella et al. 2008). MDMA's proven pro-social effects (Bedi et al. 2010) can strengthen the therapeutic alliance and may give patients the option to realize new helpful experiences in therapeutic contexts.

MDMA also enhances the release of the hormones cortisol and norepinephrine (Mas et al. 1999). These are known to trigger emotional learning, including fear extinction (Quirk and Mueller 2008).

In summary, there is a multiplicity of neurophysiologic and neurohormonal mechanisms potentially involved in the pathophysiology of PTSD and related disorders as well as in psychotherapeutic work with patients suffering from these conditions. MDMA has a range of specific effects on these pathways that together may explain MDMA's astonishing efficacy in enhancing psychotherapeutic communication and processing, not only of memories but also through allowing new reformative experiences and their durable imprinting.

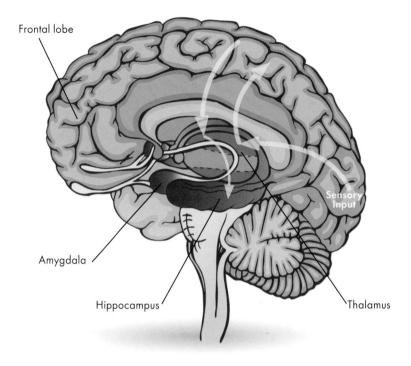

Figure 1: Normal sensory memory processing
A rough sketch of the usual neurobiological pathway in which sensory data are processed. Sensory signals come into the brain from the sensory receptors (e.g., eyes, ears) and are processed first in their specific sensory centers of the brain. They are then distributed and filtered through the thalamus. Before they are stored in the memory databank (the hippocampus) they go to parts of the neocortex for preliminary evaluation of their significance.

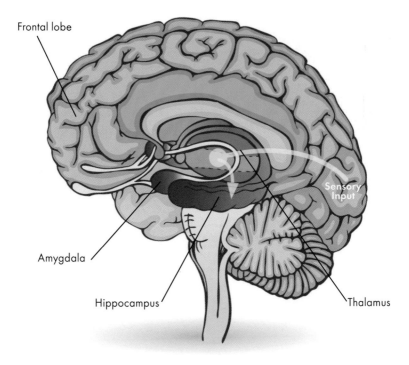

Figure 2: Traumatic sensory memory processing
The usual way in which traumatic memories are stored in the memory system. The brain system's capacity is insufficient to process and evaluate an overwhelming traumatic experience. This leads to another more primitive way of processing. Instead of being preliminarily evaluated by the neocortex, the sensory signals pass in an unselected fashion through the thalamus and are directly stored in the hippocampus. This unselected storage may explain the more or less complete and realistic re-experiencing of traumatic events during intrusive flashback memories.

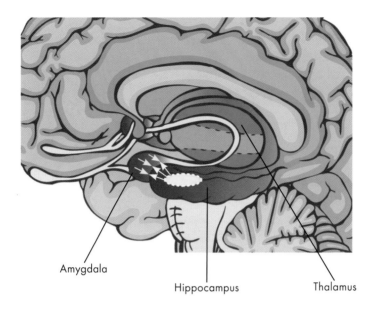

Amygdala

Hippocampus

Thalamus

Figure 3: Activated amygdala prevents traumatic memory reprocessing

If nonselected traumatic memories are stored in the hippocampus, it appears that these memories build kinds of "non-integrated" tension systems in the brain. These tension systems tend to express themselves by the involuntary retrieval of memories as seen in intrusive re-experiences and nightmares. Such involuntary and overwhelming (potentially re-traumatizing) re-experiencing are usually suppressed by the anxiety generated by the brain's fear network, including the amygdala. The result is (among others) the avoidance of stimuli associated with the originally traumatizing situation.

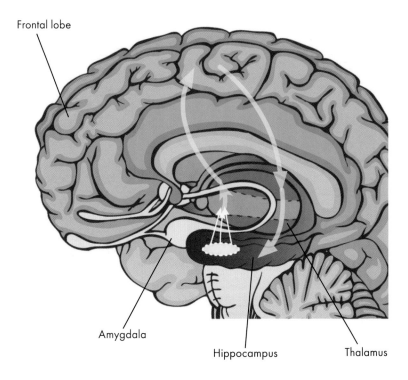

Frontal lobe

Amygdala

Hippocampus

Thalamus

Figure 4: Deactivated amygdala allows traumatic memory reprocessing
When substances like MDMA or MDE deactivate the amygdala, the memory system
is freed from the blocking effect of the brain's fear network, and the person is able to
reprocess and contextualize the relevant memories within appropriate therapy. It is
quite astonishing how entactogens engender these reformations of trauma memory
virtually without any other induction procedures. Subject material can be controlled
to a large degree by the experiencing person and helps to reintegrate formerly
non-integrated avoidance and memories that induce involuntary reexperiencing.

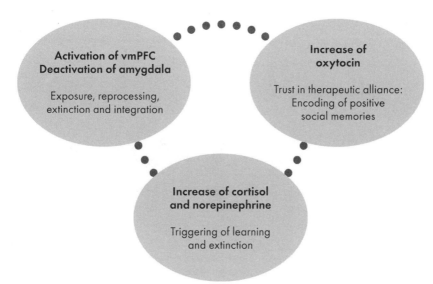

Figure 5: Neurobiological factors involved in the therapeutic potential of entactogens like MDMA.

4. Controlled studies of MDMA-assisted psychotherapy

Beginning in the 1990s, four clinical studies received permission to treat patients with MDMA-assisted psychotherapy (Doblin 2002). In 2002, Bouso et al. started a study in women with PTSD. This study couldn't be completed because of political and technical obstacles, but some positive results from the initial phase were published (Bouso et al. 2008). During the years 2004–2009 two placebo-controlled studies with patients with severe, treatment-resistant PTSD were conducted. The study by Mithoefer et al. (2011) was completed in 2009 and its results published in 2011. Twenty patients with chronic posttraumatic stress disorder, refractory both to psychotherapy and psychopharmacology, were randomly assigned to psychotherapy with concomitant active drug (n=12) or inactive placebo (n=8) administered during two eight-hour experimental psychotherapy sessions. Both groups received preparatory and follow-up non-drug psychotherapy. The primary outcome measure was the Clinician Administered PTSD Scale (CAPS), administered at baseline, four days after each experimental session, and two months after the second session. Neurocognitive testing, blood pressure, and temperature monitoring were performed. After two-month follow-up, placebo subjects were offered the option to re-enroll in the experimental procedure with open-label MDMA. Decrease in CAPS scores from baseline was significantly greater for the group who received MDMA than for the placebo group at all three time points after baseline. The rate of clinical response was 83.3% in the active treatment group and 25% in the placebo group. There were no drug-related serious adverse events, adverse neurocognitive

Substance	MDA	MDMA	MDE	MBDB
Formula				
Chemical name	Methylenedioxy-amphetamine	Methylenedioxy-methamphetamine	Methylenedioxy-ethylamphetamine	Methylamino-methylene dioxyphenylbutane
Dose (mg)	75–125	75–140	100–160	150–210
Duration of effect (hrs.)	8–10	4–6	3–5	4–6
Half-life (hrs.)	7–9	(R)-MDMA 6 (S)-MDMA 3,5	(S)-MDE 4 (R)-MDE 8	?
Effect type	entactogen/hallucinogen	entactogen	entactogen	entactogen

Table 4: Overview of the better-known entactogens (data extracted from Kraemer and Maurer 2002, Trachsel and Richard 2000, Shulgin and Shulgin 1991).

58

effects, or clinically significant blood pressure increases. The authors concluded that MDMA-assisted psychotherapy can be administered to posttraumatic stress disorder patients without evidence of harm, and it may be useful in patients who are non-responders to conventional treatments.

In 2012, Michael Mithoefer completed a study describing the results of a long-term follow-up of subjects who participated in his first MDMA/PTSD study. The long-term follow-up, conducted an average of 3.5 years after treatment, demonstrates that benefits were maintained over time. The results of the recent Swiss MDMA/PTSD study showed a clinically significant reduction of PTSD symptoms with trends toward improvement in 12 participants. These results further support the safety and efficacy of MDMA-assisted psychotherapy in patients with chronic, treatment-resistant PTSD (cf. Oehen et al. 2012). A fourth study on MDMA-assisted psychotherapy for cancer-diagnosis-related anxiety led by Halpern at Harvard's McLean Hospital has completed data with two patients to date.

5. Indications and contraindications

Psycholytic therapy is not indicated for all psychological problems or disorders amenable to psychotherapy. Published results and clinical evidence suggest that those who are particularly well-suited for a psycholytic approach are relatively ego-stable and socially competent people with anxiety, character, depressive, or sexual neuroses, and/or are afflicted with different psychosomatic disorders (Tables 5 and 6). Eating disorders like bulimia, when not too pronounced, may also be well suited to psycholytic treatment. However, it will take further clinical studies to determine the actual spectrum of treatable disorders as well as potential uses in couples therapy and for personal development in healthy people.

Diagnostic Groups	Number of Studies	Success Rate
Anxiety disorders	9	70%
Depressive disorders	4	62%
Character disorders	10	61%
Sexual neuroses	7	50%
Obsessional neuroses	10	42%
Hysterical and conversion disorders	2	31.5%
Substance dependence	6	31%

Table 5: Indications for psycholytic therapy (with hallucinogens) according to the evaluation of 42 clinical studies. (Maschner 1967)

Potentially treatable disorders	Recommended substances
Neuroses	entactogens (hallucinogens)
Psychosomatic disorders	entactogens (hallucinogens)
Bulimia nervosa	entactogens
Obsessional neuroses	entactogens
Posttraumatic stress disorder	entactogens
Alcohol dependence	hallucinogens (entactogens)
Terminal cancer patients	entactogens (hallucinogens)
Relationship disorders	entactogens
Personality disorders	entactogens (hallucinogens)

Table 6: Indications for psycholytic therapy with entactogens (modified after Passie 2007; also based on data given in Holland 2001)

When psychological instability is present (ego-structure weakness and/or borderline personality disorder, whether permanent or temporary) or when there is marked depression due to current events, it is generally contraindicated to pursue the psycholytic method. The activating effect of the substances can worsen psychological instability or depression in some individuals (Grof 1980, Leuner 1981). Such risks are clearly less pronounced in therapy using entactogens in comparison to hallucinogens. Entactogens do not usually present grave problems to patients of the indications noted in Table 5. Emotional instability and/or depressive after-swings are very rare and not pronounced. The patients themselves usually overcome such difficulties. It goes without saying that further psychotherapeutic intervention may prove necessary in any single case.

Contraindications for psycholytic therapy include those with any form of psychosis, delusional disorders, or heavy endogenous depression, and persons experiencing acute and sub-acute exacerbation of grave stress while in crisis. Other contraindications are pronounced ego-instability, severe narcissistic disorders, severe personality disorders, as well as pronounced dependency illnesses. In the case of these later ailments, a very strict indication has to be made if treatment is to proceed (Oehen 2008).

Psycholytic sessions appear to be capable of activating self-healing mechanisms. This implies that people who have relatively intact personality and good social functioning are able to benefit particularly well.

There are also medical contraindications (Table 7). Drug-drug interactions have to be clarified in each individual case. Scientific surveys evaluating complications from polypharmacy have yet to be published (e. g., Oesterheld et al. 2004). Reservations for continuing other medications should be the general rule if those substances are known to burden or induce the cytochrome-P enzyme system. Entactogens (but not hallucinogens) are metabolized via this specific enzyme system, so it may be unsafe to retain a medication that may slow or accelerate the breaking down of entactogens. A danger for serotonin syndrome is also posed by any combination of entactogens with monoamine oxidase inhibitor (MAOI) antidepressants. There is a known attenuation of entactogenic effects by serotonin reuptake inhibitors (SSRIs).

Ailments
Malignant hypertension
Seizure disorder
Severe liver disease
Severe kidney disease

Table 7: List of somatic contraindications.

6. Possible risks and complications

Long-term evaluation of thousands of patients treated using the psycholytic method during the 1950s and 1960s (mainly with LSD) indicates that this treatment can successfully be woven into the process of psychotherapy and is no more risky than conventional psychotherapy alone (Cohen 1960, Malleson 1971). As far as is known from clinical data this safety profile likely extends to the entactogens as well, because these substances induce an even more controllable altered state of consciousness (cf. contributions in Holland 2001). The possible acute and sub-acute complications of therapy involving entactogens are shown in Table 8.

Type of Complication	Frequency	Treatment
During the session		
Reactions of fear	occasional	calming influence
Disintegration of the ego in crisis	rare	psychotherapeutic stabilization
Agitation/confusion	rare	psychotherapeutic stabilization
Directly after the session		
Extended duration (hours)	very rare	further care until it wears off
Depressive fluctuations	occasional	post-care (telephone availability)
Psychological instability	occasional	psychotherapeutic stabilization

Table 8: Possible complications during and directly after psycholytic sessions with entactogens (cf. Passie 2007, also based on Naranjo 1973 and Yensen 1976)

It also has to be mentioned here that some animal and human studies suggest that MDMA/MDE may have neurotoxic potential. Such studies were done on populations of users that are part of the so-called "rave" or "techno" subculture, who are usually using these substances to enhance performance and wakefulness during all-night dance events. Nearly all of these users were taking multiple doses at one time, danced all night, and took other drugs in addition (e.g. alcohol, cannabis, amphetamines). In some of these individuals, mild neurocognitive deficits were detected in a dose-dependent fashion (for review see Gouzoulis-Mayfrank and Daumann 2006). However, how far these deficits could be attributed mainly to the taking of MDMA/MDE appeared questionable. Newer studies of these kinds of users with up to 100 cumulative ecstasy doses did not show any neurocognitive deficits (Thomasius 2000). A more recent study with users who solely used ecstasy and no additional drugs in the range of 20–150 pills showed no neurocognitive deficits (Halpern 2011). It is also noteworthy that the use of MDMA/MDE in therapeutic contexts never led to any medical complications (Gasser 1996). In summary, there is no evidence that the use of MDMA/MDE in controlled medical settings leads to acute or long-term damage in humans.

Working mechanisms of entactogens in psychotherapy

Six significant factors appear involved in the therapeutic effect of psycholytic sessions with entactogens:

1. Decrease in anxiety and psychophysical relaxation

Entactogens, such as MDMA or MDE, create a pronounced reduction in anxiety according to the descriptions dealt with here, an effect which can also be described as basal reduction in anxiety. This effect has its correlation in the neurobiological deactivation of the amygdala in the left hemisphere of the brain, an anatomical structure containing the brain's fear network. Directly connected to this reduction in anxiety is an alteration in the way the body is experienced. It is perceived as being very pleasant and free from tension. It appears as if a deep sense of wellbeing is felt, due to a very deep-reaching psychophysical relaxation (Adamson & Metzner 1988).

An important aspect of anxiety reduction is the considerable decrease in how a threat to ones own integrity is experienced, which allows new possibilities in self-perception and the recognition of problems. More often than not, the feeling of self-esteem is also profoundly changed to the positive ("I am more okay than I thought"). Many describe these changes in the experiencing of self as "opening up to love and the love of oneself." This can be understood as a temporary lifting of narcissistic blockage or dysregulation, which implies a change in the "the amounts of energy and their distribution in the mental apparatus" (Freud 1938). A judgmental inner authority found in many neurotic disorders, which condemns and hinders self-development, appears to switch off (Greer & Tolbert 1986).

Much healing succeeds through experiencing relevant feelings, in particular mourning, and is advanced through the unspecific affective activation under the substances. Occasionally, however, an affective abreaction in direct connection with the concrete experience does not occur. If so affected, the reaction of mourning (or rather the abreaction of the affects) then occurs belatedly and only after the wearing off of the acute effect of the substance (in the evening or night), a time which may also be considered part of the integration process.

2. Group experience

Regarding a group atmosphere (which provides security, a therapeutic structure, and an anxiety-reducing effect) there frequently develops an openness, calmness, and gentleness in the communication with other members of the group (an entactogen effect) all fueled by a feeling of love. Opening up and trust-building occur. Long-held interpersonal fears, reservations, and barriers may fall by the wayside (Adamson & Metzner 1988). The group then becomes an interpersonal field for trying things out, a sphere of experiment, in which corrective new experiences can be made with interhuman intimacy. Such interactions happen essentially without sexual ambitions and without interpersonal fixations after the drug effects subside. This is an astounding phenomenon and is seen time and again to enhance the sense of experimentation in the group session because new forms of intimacy and interaction can be lived out liberated from old inhibitions.

3. Acceleration of psychological processes

Entactogens and hallucinogens activate feelings. It is as if the effect of these substances works as a promoter of the patient's latent psychodynamics. Confrontation with fear, love, and not-yet-reappraised problematic relationships occur typically within the framework conditions of the therapy. The reactivation of traumatic experiences can also occur, which usually happens with inner calm and in an ordered form. Unlike other conditions or settings, the emerging (unconscious) material becomes accessible without the usual associated negativity. Instead, it offers constructive integration of that which was experienced, something normally cut off under normal consciousness. A differentiated, emotional, and intellectual clearing of the mind, and the remembering and investigation of present and past factual circumstances and relationships are possible. Also common is the gaining of an overall perspective where inner-psychological problems reside and the contexts in maintained therapeutic ego splitting. Regression is also reported, which allows for a quite realistic reliving of past events on the psychological organizational level. Also of interest is the occasional appearance thereby of alternative simulations of formative situations from the past, encapsulated in an inner realm.

Despite the similarities in the flow of the drug-assisted experience with dreaming or daydreaming, the drug-assisted experiences are out of the ordinary and intense and without dreamlike fragmentation or alienating distortions. Exaggerated forms of intrapsychological processes are rarely found within these compressed, scenic-synoptic recapitulations of essential, formative biographical events. Bound within the described intrapsychological processes, the suspicion, feeling, and recognition of one's own possibilities and resources also occur.

4. Transparency and the reduction of transference

Within the setting of the group situation, in which usually two to three therapists of both sexes are present, transference phenomena appear to play an almost marginal role. Because patients primarily concentrate on the positive security, support, and help conveyed by their therapists, and also spend most of their time concentrating on themselves (eye patches, headphones), problematic transference phenomena appear to be minimized. The propensity for transference is less activated due to the group situation and is almost completely "dissipated away."

5. Transpersonal experiences
Trust is at the forefront of transpersonal experiences with entactogens. Often a "unity with oneself" is found ("personalization" after Naranjo 1973). Mystical experience of oneness is more seldom. Even more rare are reports of revelations of archetypal correlations or fundamental questions of humanity.

Transpersonal experience can convey very deep-reaching insights, are usually very intense, and in some cases lead to a profound change in perspective about how to live and about one's values. The psychotherapeutic process often stimulates new perceptions of oneself, others, or the world, and changes viewpoints and perspectives in a way that triggers other psychotherapeutic realizations.

6. The work of integration
Lasting benefit is much more likely achieved with follow-up therapy that aims to evaluate the experiences and integrate them into everyday life. In psycholytic therapy, the first concern is the feeling, viewing, and taking on that which was perceived, followed by its integration. It goes without saying that the newly won experiences, knowledge, and access to feelings have to be discussed and processed in a careful one-on-one session because this important work for integration cannot succeed if only done on one weekend packed with such intense experiences across several individuals. If this work is not individually processed, then that which was achieved may not be effectively anchored.

Do entactogens activate powers of self-healing?

Based on the effects portrayed, in which the entactogens foster effective psychotherapeutic processes under suitably structured conditions, it is interesting to ask if change has to do with the activation of processes of self-healing. The processes playing out in the altered state of consciousness are most always coming forward into awareness independently, including otherwise unconscious processes and ways of behavior. The therapist's role during psycholytic sessions with entactogens is merely supportive and encouraging and only seldom guiding because these processes normally run "almost by themselves" and hardly ever make a more intrusive intervention necessary (Mithoefer 2008, Styk 2008). The task of the therapist is primarily in the maintenance of the framework and of a supportive manner, adapted to the energies and resources of the patient. The deep-reaching psychophysical relaxation and reduction in anxiety induced by entactogens cancel narcissistic dysregulation and distortion ("feeling of completeness," "love of oneself," "security") and thus powers of self-healing can unfold. Other relevant factors that may stimulate self-healing are transpersonal moments and insights gained by anxiety reduction and corrective new experiences in regard to one's own state as well as in the interpersonal realm.

In addition, it becomes clear from the descriptions and clinical observations that patients can constructively employ corrective new experiences (especially within the interpersonal sphere). As the LSD therapist Grof (1985: 367) notes, "a considerable by-product of this therapeutic strategy is the development of the feeling in clients that they are master over themselves. They recognize very quickly that they can help one another and that they actually are the only ones who are able to do this. In this way shrinking...the belief that only a magical intervention by the therapist... can be of use to them."

Entactogens and the four general elements of psychotherapy

In relation to the four general elements of psychotherapy as established by the internationally renowned psychotherapy researcher Grawe (2004, 1995), the following can be said based on the present study and in agreement with Schlichting's conclusions (2000: 73 f.):

> "Particularly, because not only pathology presents itself in the experience session, but also the capacity to experience feelings of love and bonding which results in intensive positive effects becoming once again perceivable by the patient. He can learn to rely on his own emotional resources to solve problems and, by means of his self-competence, also positively correct his own concept of himself. Psycholytic therapy uses problem actualization and confrontation as well, if problematic relationship patterns, anxieties, neurotic symptom formations, or defense mechanisms present themselves during the session" (translated by T.P.). This perspective deserves a special position in psycholytic treatment for its ability to improve introspection, increase insight into the psychogenesis of disorders and problems at the root of one's personal life-history, as well as one's creative potential and personal opportunities to experience." (Schlichting 2000: 74)

To summarize, psycholytic therapy, particularly with entactogens, can greatly enhance conventional psychotherapy as well as magnify relevant issues in a more therapeutically beneficial way. There are additional effects as well which have not been well researched, such as strong intrapersonal and interpersonal reductions in anxiety, altered awareness of the body, regression, hypermnestic phenomena, rescripting of past behaviors and memories of events, and transpersonal experiences. However, it has to be pointed out that clinical entactogen-assisted psychotherapy demands very high requirements in the training and experience of therapists, who must always comport themselves with good psychotherapeutic skills and a high degree of personal integrity.

References

Abramson, H.A. (ed.) (1967). *The Use of LSD in Psychotherapy and Alcoholism.* Indianapolis, New York, Kansas City: Bobbs Merrill.

Adamson, S., & Metzner, R. (1988). The nature of the MDMA experience and its role in healing, psychotherapy, and spiritual practice. *ReVision* 10: 59–72.

Auckenthaler, A. (1991). Klinische Einzelfallforschung. In: Flick, U. (ed.): *Handbuch qualitativer Sozialforschung.* München: Psychologie Verlags Union.

Bandelow, B. (2001). *Panik und Agoraphobie.* Wien: Springer.

Barolin, G.S. (1961). Erstes Europäisches Symposium für Psychotherapie unter LSD-25, Göttingen, November 1960. *Wiener Medizinische Wochenschrift,* 111: 266–68.

Bastine, R. (1992). Psychotherapie. In: Bastine, R. (ed.): *Klinische Psychologie Band 2.* Stuttgart: Kohlhammer, 179–301.

Bastine, R., Fidler, P., & Kommer, D. (1989). Was ist therapeutisch an der Psychotherapie? Versuch einer Bestandsaufnahme und Systematisierung der Psychotherapeutischen Prozessforschung. *Zeitschrift für klinische Psychologie,* 18: 3–22.

Bedi, G., Hyman, D., & de Wit, H. (2010). Is ecstasy an "Empathogen"? Effects of ±3,4-methylenedioxymethamphetamine on prosocial feelings and identification of emotional states in others. *Biological Psychiatry,* 68: 1134–40

Benz, E. (1989). *Halluzinogen–unterstützte Psychotherapie.* (Medical dissertation). Zürich: University of Zürich.

Bortz, J., & Döring, N. (1995). *Forschungsmethoden und Evaluation für Sozialwissenschaftler* (2. ed.). Berlin: Springer.

Bouso, J.C., Doblin, R., Farre, M., Alcazar, M.A., & Gomez-Jarabo, G. (2008). MDMA-assisted psychotherapy using low doses in a small sample of women with chronic posttraumatic stress disorder. *Journal of Psychoactive Drugs,* 40: 225–36.

Bradley, R., Greene, J., Russ, E., Dutra, L., & Westen, D. (2005). A multidimensional meta-analysis of psychotherapy for PTSD. *American Journal of Psychiatry,* 162: 214–23.

Buffum, J., & Moser, C. (1986). MDMA and human sexual function. *Journal of Psychoactive Drugs,* 18: 355–59.

Doblin, R. (2002). A clinical plan for MDMA (Ecstasy) in the treatment of post-traumatic stress disorder (PTSD): partnering with the FDA. *Journal of Psychoactive Drugs,* 34: 185-94.

Dürst, T. (2006). *Veränderungen im Verlauf psycholytischer Therapie aus der Sicht von Patienten.* (Diploma thesis in Psychology). Berlin: Free University of Berlin (Germany).

Dumont, G.J., Sweep, F.C., van der Steen, R., Hermsen, R., Donders, A.R., Touw, D.J., ... & Verkes, R.J. (2009). Increased oxytocin concentrations and prosocial feelings in humans after ecstasy (3,4-methylenedioxymethamphetamine) administration. *Social Neuroscience,* 4: 359–66.

Fernandez-Cerdeno, A. (1964). *Die Reaktivierung von Erlebnissen aus dem ersten Lebensjahr durch Halluzinogene (Altersregression).* (Medical dissertation). Göttingen: University of Göttingen (Germany).

Fontana, A.E. (1965). *Psicoterapia con Alucinogenos.* Buenos Aires: Editorial Losada.

Freud, S. (1964). An outline of psycho-analysis (1938). In: Freud, S.: *The Standard Edition of the Complete Psychological Works of Sigmund Freud Vol. XXIII.* London: The Hogarth Press, 182.

Gamma, A., Buck, A., Berthold, T., & Liechti, M.E., & Vollenweider, F.X. (2000). 3,4-Methylenedioxymethamphetamine (MDMA) modulates cortical and limbic brain activity as measured by [H(2)(15)O]-PET in healthy humans. *Neuropsychopharmacology,* 23: 388–95.

Gasser, P. (1996). Die psycholytische Psychotherapie in der Schweiz von 1988–1993. *Schweizer Archiv für Neurologie und Psychiatrie,* 147: 59–65.

George, M.S., Ketter, T.A., Parekh, P.I., Horwitz, B., Herscovitch, P., & Post, R.M. (1995). Brain activity during transient sadness and happiness in healthy women. *American Journal of Psychiatry,* 152: 341–51.

Gouzoulis-Mayfrank, E., & Daumann, J. (2006). Neurotoxicity of methylenedioxyamphetamines (MDMA; ecstasy) in humans: how strong is the evidence for persistent brain damage? *Addiction,* 101: 348–61.

Gouzoulis-Mayfrank, E., Hermle, L., Kovar, K.A., & Sass, H. (1996). Die Entaktogene Ecstasy (MDMA), Eve (MDE) und andere ringsubstituierte Amphetaminderivate. Eine neue Substanzklasse unter den illegalen Designerdrogen? *Nervenarzt,* 67: 369–80.

Grawe, K. (1995). Grundriss einer Allgemeinen Psychotherapie. *Psychotherapeut,* 40: 130–45.

Grawe, K. (2004). Psychological Therapy. Göttingen et al.: Hogrefe.

Green, A.R., Mechan, A.O., Elliott, J.M., O'Shea, E., & Colado, M.I. (2003). The Pharmacology and clinical pharmacology 3,4-methylenedioxymethamphetamine (MDMA, "ecstasy"). *Pharmacological Reviews,* 55: 463–508.

Greenberg, L.S., & Rice, L.N. (eds.) (1984). *Patterns of Change.* New York: Guilford.

Greer, G., & Tolbert, R. (1986). Subjective reports of the effects of MDMA in a clinical setting. *Journal of Psychoactive Drugs,* 18: 319–27.

Griffiths, R.R., Richards, W.A., McCann, U., & Jesse, R. (2006). Psilocybin can occasion mystical-type experiences having substantial and sustained personal meaning and spiritual significance. *Psychopharmacology,* 187: 268–83.

Grof, S. (1975). *Realms of the Human Unconscious.* New York: Viking.

Grof, S. (1980). *LSD-psychotherapy.* Pomona, CA: Hunter House.

Grof, S. (1985). *Beyond the Brain: Birth, Death and Transcendence in Psychotherapy.* Albany, NY: State University of New York Press.

Grof S, Grof, C. (2010). *Holotropic Breathwork.* New York: State University of New York Press.

Guastella, A.J., Mitchell P.B., & Mathews, F. (2008). Oxytocin enhances the encoding of positive social memories in humans. *Biological Psychiatry,* 64: 256–58.

Halpern, J.H., Sherwood, A.R., Hudson, J.I., Gruber, S., Kozin, D., & Pope, H.G. Jr. (2011). Residual neurocognitive features of long-term ecstasy users with minimal exposure to other drugs. *Addiction,* 106: 777–86.

Hess, P. (1997). Therapie mit Entaktogenen. In: Neumeyer, J., Schmidt-Semisch, H. (eds.): Ecstasy– Design für die Seele? Heidelberg: Lambertus, 189–203.

Holland, J. (ed.) *Ecstasy: The Complete Guide.* Rochester: Park Street Press.

Johansen, P.O., & Krebs, T.S. (2009) How could MDMA (ecstasy) help anxiety disorders? A neurobiological rationale. *Journal of Psychopharmacology,* 23: 389–91.

Jungaberle, H., Gasser, P., Weinhold, J., & Verres, R. (eds.) (2008) *Psychotherapie mit Psychoaktiven Substanzen.* Bern, Stuttgart, Toronto: Hans Huber.

Komisaruk, B.R., & Whipple, B. (2005). Functional MRI of the brain during orgasm in women. *Annual Review of Sex Research,* 16: 62–86.

Kraemer, T., Maurer, H.H. (2002). Toxicokinetics of amphetamines: metabolism and toxi-cokinetic data of designer drugs, amphetamine, methamphetamine, and their N-alkyl derivatives. *Therapeutic Drug Monitoring,* 24: 277–89.

Kris, E. (1974). *Psychoanalytic Explorations in Art.* New York: Schocken Books.

Langenmayr, A., & Kosfelder, J. (1995). Methodische Entscheidungen in der Evaluation von Psychotherapie. *Zeitschrift für Klinische Psychologie, Psychopathologie und Psychotherapie,* 43: 273–90.

Legewie, H. (1994). Globalauswertung von Dokumenten. In: Böhm, A., Muhr, T., & Mengel, A. (eds.), Texte verstehen: Konzepte, Methoden, Werkzeuge. Konstanz: Universitätsverlag, 177–82.

Leuner, H. (1962). *Die Experimentelle Psychose.* Berlin, Göttingen, Heidelberg: Springer.

Leuner, H. (1971). *Halluzinogene in der Psychotherapie. Pharmakopsychiatrie, Neuro-Psychopharmakologie,* 4: 333–51.

Leuner, H. (1981). *Halluzinogene.* Bern, Stuttgart, Wien: Huber.

Liberzon, I., & Sripada, C.S. (2008). The functional neuroanatomy of PTSD: a critical review. *Progress in Brain Research,* 167: 151–69.

Lienert, G.A. (1964). *Belastung und Regression*. Meisenheim: Anton Hain.

Liester, M.B., Grob, C.S., Bravo, G.L., Walsh, R.N. (1992). Phenomenology and sequelae of 3,4-methylenedioxymethamphetamine use. *Journal of Nervous and Mental Disease*, 180: 345-52.

Mas, M., Farré, M., de la Torre, R., Roset, P.N., Ortuño, J., Segura, J., & Camí, J. (1999). Cardiovascular and neuroendocrine effects and pharmacokinetics of 3,4-methyl-enedioxymethamphetamine in humans. *Journal of Pharmacology and Experimental Therapeutics*, 290: 136-45.

Mascher, E. (1967). Psycholytic therapy: statistics and indications. In: Brill, H. (ed.): *Neuro-Psycho-Pharmacology*. Amsterdam, New York, London, Milan, Tokyo, Buenos Aires: Excerpta Medica, 441-44.

Masters, R.E.L., & Houston, J. (1966). *The Varieties of Psychedelic Experience*. New York: Holt, Rhinehart & Winston.

Mayring, P. (2000). *Qualitative Inhaltsanalyse. Grundlagen und Techniken*. 7. ed. Weinheim: Deutscher Studien Verlag.

McGothlin, W., Cohen, & S., McGothlin, M.S. (1967). Long lasting effects of LSD on normals. *Archives of General Psychiatry*, 17: 521-31.

McNally, R.J. (2007). Mechanisms of exposure therapy: how neuroscience can improve psychological treatments for anxiety disorders. *Clinical Psychology Review*, 27: 750-59.

Mithoefer, M. (2008). MDMA bei der Behandlung posttraumatischer Belastungsstörungen. In: Jungaberle, H., Gasser, P., Weinhold, J., & Verres, R. (eds.) *Psychotherapie mit psychoaktiven Substanzen*. Bern, Stuttgart, Toronto: Hans Huber, 195-222.

Mithoefer, M.C., Wagner, M.T., Mithoefer, A.T., Jerome, I., & Doblin, R. (2011). The safety and efficacy of (+/-)3,4-methylendioxymethamphetamine-assisted psychotherapy in subjects with chronic, treatment-resistant posttraumatic stress disorder: the first randomized controlled pilot study. *Journal of Psychopharmacology*, 25: 439-52.

Moustakas, C. (1994). *Phenomenological Research Methods*. Thousand Oaks, London, New Delhi: SAGE Publications.

Naranjo, C. (1973). *The Healing Journey*. New York: Pantheon.

Nichols, D. (1986) Differences between the mechanisms of action of MDMA, MBDB and the classic hallucinogens. Identification of a new therapeutic class: Entactogens. *Journal of Psychoactive Drugs*, 18: 305-11.

Nutt, D.J., Malizia, A.L. (2004). Structural and functional brain changes in posttraumatic stress disorder. *Journal of Clinical Psychiatry*, 65 (Suppl. 1): 11-17.

Oehen, P. (2008). Indikationen und Kontraindikationen der Substanz-unterstützten Psychotherapie. In: : Jungaberle, H., Gasser,P., Weinhold, J., Verres, R. (eds.). *Psychotherapie mit psychoaktiven Substanzen*. Bern, Stuttgart, Toronto: Hans Huber, 131-46.

Pagani, M., Högberg, G., Salmaso, D., Nardo, D., Sundin, O., Jonsson, C. ... & Häll-ström, T. (2007). Effects of EMDR psychotherapy on 99mTc-HMPAO distribution in occupation-related post-traumatic stress disorder. *Nuclear Medicine Communications*, 28: 757-65.

Pahnke, W.N., & Richards, W.A. (1966). Implications of LSD and experimental mysticism. *Journal of Religion and Health*, 5: 175-208.

Passie, T. (1997). *Psycholytic and psychedelic therapy research 1931-1995: A complete international bibliography.* Hannover: Laurentius Publishers.

Passie, T. (2007). Contemporary psychedelic therapy: An overview. In: Winkelman, M.J., Roberts, T.B. (eds.): *Psychedelic medicine Vol. 1.* Westport, London: Praeger, 45-68.

Passie, T., Hartmann, U., Schneider, U., Emrich, H.M. (2005a). Was sind Entaktogene? Pharmakologische und psychopharmakologische Aspekte einer Substanzgruppe. *Suchtmedizin*, 7: 235-45.

Passie, T., Dürst, T. (2008). Heilungsprozesse im veränderten Bewusstsein: Elemente psy-cholytischer Therapieerfahrung aus der Sicht von Patienten. In: Jungaberle, H., Gasser, P., Weinhold, J., & Verres, R. (eds.): *Psychotherapie mit psychoaktiven Substanzen.* Bern, Stuttgart, Toronto: Hans Huber, 165-94.

Passie, T., Hartmann, U., Schneider, U., & Krüger, T.H.C. (2005b). Ecstasy (MDMA) mimics the post-orgasmic state: impairment of sexual drive and function during acute MDMA-effects may be due to increased prolactin secretion. *Medical Hypotheses*, 64: 899-903.

Quirk, G.J., & Mueller, D. (2008). Neural mechanisms of extinction learning and retrieval. *Neuropsychopharmacology*, 33: 56-72.

Schlichting, M. (2000). Wirkfaktoren der Psycholytischen Therapie. In: Schlichting, M. (ed.): Welten des Bewusstseins Bd. 10. Berlin: *Verlag für Wissenschaft und Bildung*, 67-76.

Scott, J.A. (1993). *Hypnoanalysis for Individual and Marital Psychotherapy.* New York, London, Sydney, Toronto: Gardner Press.

Seymour, R.B. (1986). *MDMA.* San Francisco: Haight Ashbury Publications.

Sherwood, J.N., Stolaroff, M.J., Harman, W.W. (1962). The psychedelic experience—A new concept in psychotherapy. *Journal of Neuropsychiatry* 4: 69-80.

Shin, L.M., Wright, C.I., Cannistraro, P.A., Wedig, M.M., McMullin, K., Martis, B., Mack-lin, M.L., ... & Rauch, S.L. (2005). A functional magnetic resonance imaging study of amygdala and medial prefrontal cortex responses to overtly presented fearful faces in posttraumatic stress disorder. *Archives of General Psychiatry*, 62: 273-81.

Shulgin, A.T., & Shulgin, A. (1991). *PIHKAL: a chemical love story.* Berkeley: Transform Press.

Simon, N.M., Connor, K.M., Lang, A.J., Rauch, S., Krulewicz, S., Lebeau, R.T. ... & Pollack, M.H. (2008). Paroxetine CR augmentation for posttraumatic stress disorders refrac-tory to prolonged exposure therapy. *Journal of Clinical Psychiatry*, 69: 400-5.

Spencer, A.M. (1963). Permissive group therapy with lysergic acid diethylamide. British Journal of Psychiatry, 109: 37–45.

Styk, J. (1994). Rückblick auf die letzten sieben Jahre der Schweizerischen Ärztegesellschaft für Psycholytische Therapie (SÄPT). In: Dittrich, A., Hofmann, A., & Leuner, H. (eds.). Welten des Bewußtseins Band 4. Berlin: Verlag für Wissenschaft und Bildung, 149–54.

Styk, J. (1997). MDMA-Therapie in der Schweiz. In: Neumeyer, J., & Schmidt-Semisch, H. (eds.) Ecstasy – Design füer die Seele? Freiburg/Br.: Lambertus, 204–10.

Styk, J. (2008). Personal communication.

Thomasius, R. (2000). Ecstasy. Stuttgart: Wissenschaftliche Verlagsgesellschaft.

Vollenweider, F.X. (2001). Brain mechanisms of hallucinogens and entactogens. Dialogues in Clinical Neuroscience, 3: 265–79.

WHO Expert Committee on Drug Dependence (1985). Twenty-second report. Technical Report Series #729. Geneva: World Health Organization.

Widmer, S. (1997). Listening into the Heart of Things. Lusslingen: Basic Editions

Winkelman, M.J., & Roberts, T.B. (eds.) (2007). Psychedelic medicine Vol. 1 & 2. Westport, London: Praeger.

Witzel, A. (1982). Verfahren der Qualitativen Sozialforschung: Überblick und Alternativen. Frankfurt am Main: Campus.

Witzel, A. (1985). Das problemzentrierte Interview. In: Jüttemann, G. (ed.): Qualitative Forschung in der Psychologie, 227–55. Weinheim: Beltz.

Witzel, A. (2000). Das problemzentrierte Interview. Forum Qualitative Sozialforschung / Forum: Qualitative Social Research 1(1) [Online Journal], accessible: http://www.qualitative-research.net/index.php/fqs/article/view/1132.

Zegans, L.S., Pollard, J.C., & Brown, D. (1967). The effects of LSD-25 on creativity and tolerance to regression. Archives of General Psychiatry, 16: 740–9.

Zemishlany, Z., Aizenberg, D., & Weizman, A. (2001). Subjective effects of MDMA ('Ecstasy') on human sexual function. European Psychiatry, 16: 127–30.

Appendices

Appendix 1: Concept and method of the interview study

How and to what extent do patients, from their point of view, experience changes in the psychotherapeutic process when it is supported by MDMA or MDE? We present our evaluation with the intent to isolate those factors (occurring in psycholytic group sessions) which the patients experienced as particularly helpful and effective in resolving their problems.

Qualitative data was collected in our study. This kind of research is devoted to looking at the psychotherapeutic process as perceived by the subject undergoing it. When looking at relationships between therapeutic intervention and therapeutic change, this kind of process-oriented research (in distinction to so-called outcome-oriented research) has grown in importance since the mid-1980s. It was intended to shed light on the conditions required for a successful course of therapy (Bastine 1992). Thus, the therapeutic process became the subject of detailed research into changes, with the aim of identifying those factors decisive for the therapeutic changes, as well as how factors interact (Bastine et al. 1989, Greenberg and Rice 1984).

For the description of structure and dynamics of change in process-oriented psychotherapy research, case study research has established a special role (Auckenthaler 1991). Case studies allow "...one to look more intensively and to use more examination material, through the concentration on one object of scrutiny or relatively few people" (Witzel 1982: 78, Langenmayer and Kosfelder 1995).

Semi-structured interviews with patients lasting approximately two hours were held. The connecting thread consisted usually of eight questions. The data were obtained using the paradigm of the problem-centered interview according to Witzel (1985, 2000). Data evaluation was completed on one hand following global evaluation (Bortz & Döring 1995, Legewie, 1994), and on the other hand with qualitative content analysis after Mayring (2000), as done in the original diploma thesis (Dürst 2006).

In the preceding text of this book, the ways things were experienced and the contents of experiences under the effects of the entactogens are presented and analyzed. The type of presentation and analysis isn't a content analysis as used in the original diploma thesis by Dürst (2006). Instead, it used an approach based on the phenomenological method (cf. Moustakas 1994). This approach uses statements from interviewed subjects describing their experience and selects material while avoiding a preselection criteria that is often implied by preceding theoretical frameworks. For this work, representative passages of the interviews were selected and grouped in clusters that represent typical subjective experiences in order to demonstrate common forms and contents of experiences in psycholytic therapy as well as processes that imply changes in the patient's behavior and experience. After this, the most representative passages were, analyzed, contextualized in a theoretical framework, and integrated into a coherent text.

Appendix 2: Psycholytic group session (scheme)

Group size of at least six to eight, optimum of 10–15, maximum 20 participants.

Staff ratio of around one member per four to five participants (at least one female).

The setting should be light, homey rooms with pictures and works of art. There should be enough mattresses and cushions for each person to be comfortable.

"L" ("LSD"): normally 100–150 mcg, but also individually 150–300 mcg.

"M" ("MDMA"): normally 150 mg. If necessary, an additional 50 mg can be administered (only 90–50 min. after taking the initial dose).

Have acetaminophen (paracetamol) available for headaches (tablets and suppositories).

Each person should have headphones for individual use.

Each person should have eyeshades for use when breathing and throughout the session ("to look inwards").

Friday

☐ 19.00: Meeting begins. Allow 30 minutes for introductions.

☐ 19.30: Start

☐ Short induction of trance: "Silence" to begin, then shaking exercises for 20 minutes (e.g., such as the CD by Deuter: "Kundalini"),
Turn music off. All remain standing quietly for about 5 min. ("self awareness"). Afterwards breathe in deeply, look around and choose a partner for the next exercise.

☐ Individuals formulate personal issue with a partner. Allow two or three rounds for each group of two (2x10 min. per round). One focuses on his issue while the other simply listens. At the end of each round: Concentrate your thoughts again: What will it be about? Find a summarizing, closing sentence.

☐ Each person presents his or her focused personal issue to the group (between 5 and 20 min. per person). Therapists offer individual therapeutic support.

☐ Decide on the substance for therapy with patient.

☐ 22.30: Food, eaten together up until ca. 23.00.

Saturday

☐ 09.00: Start without breakfast.

☐ Explain the principles and safe nature of holotropic breathwork according to Grof and Grof (2010) (including the side effects) and the possible experiences that it offers for the trip. Distribute eye patches.

☐ All participate in forced, music-supported hyperventilation with light encouragement from the therapists (general "urging on" and individual tips) for approximately 60 min. followed by a 30 min. relaxation phase

☐ Everyone writes down experiences had during the hyperventilation.

☐ Statement given after the breathing exercise: Let your breathing experience pass by in your mind once again. It has to do with your journey. Make notes if you wish.

☐ Afterwards, place the mattresses out in the room ready for use.

☐ Form a circle. Each member of the group briefly describes his/her experiences in the breathing session. Define a possible thematic emphasis stemming from the current group (e.g. anxiety about mother's judgments) to which therapists can then say something which characterizes it.

☐ Still in the circle: Everyone holds hands: Feel your energy and the energy of the group and how it carries you. Reference to the signal system: Anyone raising a hand signals the need for help or to talk; also personally preferred staff can be called for.
Administer substance between 11.00 and 12.00. Then, allow approximately 10 minutes of free general and personal conversation by the group. Announce that the start is due in around 15 minutes. (Everyone should lie down quietly at his or her place by then.)

☐ Fifteen minutes after substance administration: Ensure that all participants are lying down quietly in their own spaces. Everyone should be quiet now and keep to him or herself. Is everything OK?

☐ Rest phase without music for approximately 10 minutes.

☐ The initiation into the experience follows 25 minutes after administration: Breathe in and out deeply. In and out (three to five times). Your chest is expanding. Feel it, feel it yourself as you are doing it. In and out, in and out, in and out. If you carry on this breathing, you may feel a profound contact with yourself – maybe you will also feel your heart with the same quality, one which says yes and not always only fight, one which can also let be. Above all is also the quality of this yes voice to yourself, the acceptance. Speak this out with your yes – your life energy is in this, too. Maybe there is a small no, which is stopping you from saying your yes. Just say no. Where does my no lead to? Try it out: Maybe your no will lead you directly to your journey.

☐ Beginning of the journey: put on headphones and eye patches and start the music.

☐ Individual assistance by therapists is available as necessary for the next six to seven hours. All participants should remain on their mattresses if possible; however, with little strictness.

☐ Between 18.00 and 19.00 (before food break) three assistants make a "final round" in order to ask: Where are you now and what could still be there for you?

☐ Offer food at around 19.00.

☐ At 20.00 the group is by itself for further introspection, exchanges, snuggling up, etc.

Sunday

☐ Sart at 09.00

☐ Large communal breakfast.

☐ Dancing takes place to a five-minute piece of rhythmic, loosening-up, and stimulating music played loudly.

☐ The integration hour begins between 10.00 and 10.30. Each person talks in front of the group about his journey: How they experienced and what they experienced, what was the result and above all: How much of this can definitely be translated into everyday life and how (5 to 30 min. per participant).

☐ One to two tea breaks (depending on size of group). End the integration round at 14.00 up to 15.00.

☐ Remind the group of the importance of making a written record of their experiences.

☐ Farewells.

About the Publisher

Founded in 1986, the Multidisciplinary Association for Psychedelic Studies (MAPS) is an IRS-approved 501(c)(3) non-profit research and educational organization. You can learn more about our work at www.maps.org.

For more about treating PTSD with MDMA-assisted psychotherapy, visit www.mdmaptsd.org.

MAPS works to create medical, legal, and cultural contexts for people to benefit from the careful uses of psychedelics and marijuana. MAPS furthers its mission by

- Developing psychedelics and marijuana into prescription medicines
- Training therapists and working to establish a network of treatment centers
- Supporting scientific research into spirituality, creativity, and neuroscience
- Educating the public honestly about the risks and benefits of psychedelics and marijuana.

Our top priority research project is our international series of Phase 2 clinical studies into the safety and efficacy of MDMA-assisted psychotherapy for posttraumatic stress disorder (PTSD). Data from these studies will lay the groundwork for larger multi-site studies intended to make MDMA-assisted psychotherapy a legal, FDA-approved treatment for PTSD. With promising results and growing support from medical and therapeutic professionals, the main challenge is to raise the funds necessary to support this vital research.

At the time of this publication, there is no funding available for these studies from governments, pharmaceutical companies, or major foundations. That means that—at least for now—the future of psychedelic and marijuana research rests in the hands of individual donors.

Please join MAPS in supporting the expansion of scientific knowledge in the promising area of psychedelic research. Progress is only possible with the support of those who care enough to take individual and collective action.

How MAPS Has Made a Difference

Since 1986, MAPS has distributed over $12 million to research and educational projects in accordance with its mission. These include:

- Sponsoring the first study in the U.S. to evaluate MDMA's therapeutic applications for subjects with chronic, treatment-resistant posttraumatic stress disorder (PTSD). This study found that 83% of those treated with MDMA-assisted psychotherapy no longer qualified for a diagnosis of PTSD following treatment, and that those benefits were sustained for an average of 3½ years. These results were published in the Journal of Psychopharmacology (Mithoefer et al. 2010, 2012).
- Planning or conducting additional studies of MDMA-assisted psychotherapy for PTSD in Canada, Australia, Switzerland, Israel, Jordan, and the United Kingdom.
- Hosting three major conferences on psychedelic research—Psychedelic Science in the 21st Century (2010), Cartographie Psychedelica (2011), and Psychedelic Science 2013 (2013). Psychedelic Science in the 21st Century was the largest conference on psychedelic science in nearly 40 years. The widespread positive attention it received from international news media—including The New York Times, CNN, USA Today, BBC, and Scientific American—was a turning point in the return of psychedelics to mainstream science and culture.
- Sponsoring an ongoing Phase 2 pilot study of MDMA-assisted psychotherapy for veterans of war with PTSD. At the time of this publication, the study has treated eight out of 24 subjects in Charleston, SC.
- Completing the first clinical study of LSD in humans since 1972. The study explored the effectiveness of this form of therapy for patients suffering from anxiety associated with terminal illness. At the time of this publication, a paper describing the results is awaiting publication in a peer-reviewed scientific journal.
- Designing a study of smoked or vaporized marijuana as a treatment for symptoms of PTSD in U.S. veterans of war. The study will evaluate the safety and efficacy of several different strains of botanical marijuana. At the time of this publication, the federal government is blocking this research from moving forward by refusing to supply the marijuana necessary to conduct the study.
- Supporting a federal lawsuit against the U.S. Drug Enforcement Administration by Prof. Lyle Craker for refusing to grant him a license for a MAPS-sponsored medical marijuana production facility at the University of Massachusetts-Amherst. At the time of this publication, we are awaiting a decision from the United States Court of Appeals for the First Circuit in Lyle E. Craker v. Drug Enforcement Administration (2012).
- Sponsoring an international series of observational studies of ibogaine-assisted therapy for addiction.
- Supporting long-term follow-up studies of early research on LSD and psilocybin from the 1950s and 1960s.

- Sponsoring Dr. Evgeny Krupitsky's pioneering research into the use of ketamine-assisted psychotherapy in the treatment of alcoholism and heroin addiction.
- Assisting Dr. Charles Grob to obtain permission for the first human studies in the U.S. with MDMA after it was criminalized in 1985.
- Sponsoring the first study analyzing the purity and potency of street samples of ecstasy and marijuana.
- Funding Dr. Donald Abrams' successful efforts to obtain permission for the first study of the therapeutic use of marijuana in humans in 15 years, and to secure a $1 million grant from the U.S. National Institute on Drug Abuse.
- Obtaining orphan-drug designation from the U.S. Food and Drug Administration for smoked marijuana in the treatment of AIDS wasting syndrome.
- Funding the synthesis of psilocybin for the first U.S. FDA-approved clinical trial of psilocybin in 25 years.
- Sponsoring psychedelic harm reduction programs and services at community events, festivals, schools, and churches.

Why Donate?

When you contribute to MAPS, you help make a world where psychedelics and marijuana are safely and legally available for beneficial uses, and where research is governed by rigorous scientific evaluation of their risks and benefits.

If you contribute $25 or more, you will receive the tri-annual *MAPS Bulletin*. The Bulletin contains the latest in worldwide psychedelic and medical marijuana research, as well as feature articles, visionary art, personal accounts, and book reviews. If you contribute $75 or more, you will receive your choice of one of MAPS' published books.

Your donation will be used to fund our highest-priority projects. Donations are tax-deductible as allowed by law, and may be made by credit card or personal check (made out to MAPS). Gifts of stock are also welcome, and MAPS encourages supporters to include MAPS in their will or estate plans.

MAPS takes your privacy seriously. The MAPS e-mail list is strictly confidential and will not be shared with other organizations. The MAPS Bulletin is mailed in a plain white envelope.

For more information or to join our online mailing list please visit our website at **www.maps.org**.

MAPS
309 Cedar Street #2323, Santa Cruz CA 95060
Phone: 831-429-MDMA (6362) • Fax: 831-429-6370
E-mail: askmaps@maps.org • Web: www.maps.org

More Books Published by MAPS

Ayahuasca Religions: A Comprehensive Bibliography & Critical Essays
by Beatriz Caiuby Labate, Isabel Santana de Rose,
and Rafael Guimarães dos Santos
translated by Matthew Meyer
ISBN: 978-0-9798622-1-2 $11.95
The last few decades have seen a broad expansion of the ayahuasca religions, and (especially since the millennium) an explosion of studies into the spiritual uses of ayahuasca. *Ayahuasca Religions* grew out of the need for a catalogue of the large and growing list of titles related to this subject, and offers a map of the global literature. Three researchers located in different cities (Beatriz Caiuby Labate in São Paulo, Rafael Guimarães dos Santos in Barcelona, and Isabel Santana de Rose in Florianópolis, Brazil) worked in a virtual research group for a year to compile a list of bibliographical references on Santo Daime, Barquinha, the União do Vegetal (UDV), and urban ayahuasqueiros. The review includes specialized academic literature as well as esoteric and experiential writings produced by participants of ayahuasca churches.

Drawing it Out
by Sherana Harriet Francis
ISBN: 0-9669919-5-8 $19.95
Artist Sherana Francis' fascinating exploration of her LSD psychotherapy experience contains a series of 61 black-and white illustrations along with accompanying text. The book documents the author's journey through a symbolic death and rebirth, with powerful surrealist self-portraits of her psyche undergoing transformation. Francis' images unearth universal experiences of facing the unconscious as they reflect her personal struggle towards healing. An 8.5-by-11 inch paperback with an introduction by Stan Grof, this makes an excellent coffee table book.

Honor Thy Daughter
By Marilyn Howell, Ed.D.
ISBN: 0-9798622-6-4 $16.95
This is an intimate true story by Marilyn Howell, Ed.D., about her family's search for physical, emotional, and spiritual healing as her daughter struggles with terminal cancer. The family's journey takes them through the darkest corners of corporate medicine, the jungles of Brazil, the pallid hallways of countless hospitals, and ultimately into the hands of an anonymous therapist who offers the family hope and healing through MDMA-assisted psychotherapy. The story was originally featured in a 2006 Boston Globe article entitled "A Good Death" in which Howell's identity was concealed. With psychedelic medicine increasingly a part of the mainstream vocabulary, in this poignant new book Howell comes out of the closet and shares with us how psychedelic therapy helped heal the bonds ripped apart by illness.

Ketamine: Dreams and Realities
by Karl Jansen, M.D., Ph.D.
ISBN: 0-9660019-7-4 $14.95
London researcher Dr. Karl Jansen has studied ketamine at every level, from photographing the receptors to which ketamine binds in the human brain to observing the similarities between the psychoactive effects of the drug and near-death experiences. He writes about ketamine's potential as an adjunct to psychotherapy, as well as about its addictive nature and methods of treating addiction. Jansen is the world's foremost expert on ketamine, and this is a great resource for anyone who wishes to understand ketamine's effects, risks, and potential.

LSD: My Problem Child
by Albert Hofmann, Ph.D. (4th English edition, paperback)
ISBN: 978-0-9798622-2-9 $15.95
This is the story of LSD told by a concerned yet hopeful father. Organic chemist Albert Hofmann traces LSD's path from a promising psychiatric research medicine to a recreational drug sparking hysteria and prohibition. We follow Hofmann's trek across Mexico to discover sacred plants related to LSD and listen as he corresponds with other notable figures about his remarkable discovery. Underlying it all is Dr. Hofmann's powerful conclusion that mystical experience may be our planet's best hope for survival. Whether induced by LSD, meditation, or arising spontaneously, such experiences help us to comprehend "the wonder, the mystery of the divine in the microcosm of the atom, in the macrocosm of the spiral nebula, in the seeds of plants, in the body and soul of people." More than sixty years after the birth of Albert Hofmann's "problem child," his vision of its true potential is more relevant—and more needed—than ever. The eulogy that Dr. Hofmann wrote himself and was read by his children at his funeral is the forward to the 4th edition.

LSD Psychotherapy
by Stanislav Grof, M.D. (4th Edition, Paperback)
ISBN: 0-9798622-0-5 $19.95
LSD Psychotherapy is a complete study of the use of LSD in clinical therapeutic practice, written by the world's foremost LSD psychotherapist. The text was written as a medical manual and as a historical record portraying a broad therapeutic vision. It is a valuable source of information for anyone wishing to learn more about LSD. The therapeutic model also extends to other substances: the MAPS research team used LSD Psychotherapy as a key reference for its first MDMA/PTSD study. Originally published in 1980, this 2008 paperback edition has a new introduction by Albert Hofmann, Ph.D., a forward by Andrew Weil, M.D., and color illustrations.

The Secret Chief Revealed
by Myron Stolaroff
ISBN: 0-9669919-6-6 $12.95
The second edition of *The Secret Chief* is a collection of interviews with "Jacob," the underground psychedelic therapist who is revealed years after his death as psychologist Leo Zeff. Before his death in 1988, Zeff provided psychedelic therapy to over 3,000 people. As "Jacob," he relates the origins of his early interest in psychedelics, how he chose his clients, and what he did to prepare them. He discusses the dynamics of the individual and group trip, the characteristics and appropriate dosages of various drugs, and the range of problems that people worked through. Stanislav Grof, Ann and Alexander Shulgin, and Albert Hofmann each contribute writings about the importance of Leo's work. In this new edition, Leo's family and former clients also write about their experiences with him. This book is an easy-to-read introduction to the techniques and potential of psychedelic therapy.

The Ultimate Journey: Consciousness and the Mystery of Death
By Stanislav Grof, M.D., Ph.D. (2nd edition)
ISBN: 0-9660019-9-0 $19.95
Dr. Stanislav Grof, author of *LSD Psychotherapy* and originator of Holotropic Breathwork, offers a wealth of perspectives on how we can enrich and transform the experience of dying in our culture. This 356-page book features 40 pages of images (24 in color) and a foreword by Huston Smith. Grof discusses his own patients' experiences of death and rebirth in psychedelic therapy, investigates cross-cultural beliefs and paranormal and near-death research, and argues that contrary to the predominant Western perspective death is not necessarily the end of consciousness. Grof is a psychiatrist with over forty years of experience with research into non-ordinary states of consciousness and one of the founders of transpersonal psychology. He is the founder of the International Transpersonal Association, and has published over 140 articles in professional journals. The latest edition of *The Ultimate Journey* includes a new foreword by David Jay Brown, M.A., and Peter Gasser, M.D.

Shipping and Handling

Shipping varies by weight of books. Approximate costs for shipping one book are:

- Domestic priority mail (allow 4–7 days): $7.00
- Domestic media mail (allow 2–4 weeks): $4.00
- First-class international mail (allow 2–3 weeks): varies by country

Bulk orders are welcome. Please contact MAPS for details.

Books can be purchased online by visiting www.maps.org (credit card or Paypal), over the phone by calling 831-429-MDMA (6362), or by visiting your favorite local bookstore.

You may also send orders by mail to:

MAPS
309 Cedar Street #2323
Santa Cruz, CA, 95060
Phone: 831-429-MDMA (6362)
Fax: 831-429-6370
E-mail: orders@maps.org
www.maps.org

TORSTEN PASSIE, M.D.

About the author

Torsten Passie, M.D., M.A., is Professor of Psychiatry and Psychotherapy at Hannover Medical School (Germany) where he serves as the Director of the Laboratory for Neurocognition and Consciousness. He is currently Visiting Professor at Harvard Medical School. Dr. Passie also serves on the Board of Directors of the Swiss Physicians Society for Psycholytic Therapy (SAePT).

Dr. Passie received his M.A. in philosophy and sociology from Leibniz University of Hannover, and his M.D. from Hannover Medical School. Dr. Passie has worked in the field of altered states of consciousness for more than 20 years, studying with Professor Hanscarl Leuner (Göttingen University, Germany) and Professor Hinderk M. Emrich (Hannover Medical School, Germany).

Dr. Passie has conducted extensive research on the psychophysiology of altered states of consciousness, and is a leading European expert on the pharmacology and therapeutic use of psychedelic drugs. He has done clinical research with cannabinoids, ketamine, nitrous oxide, and psilocybin.

His work has been published in the *Journal of Psychopharmacology, Psychosomatic Medicine, Addiction, Neuropsychobiology, Addiction Biology, CNS Neuroscience and Therapeutics*, and others.

Books

The Pharmacology of LSD
by Annelie Hintzen, M.D., and Torsten Passie, M.D.
Oxford University Press: 2010

Psycholytic and Psychedelic Therapy Research 1931–1995:
A Complete International Bibliography
by Torsten Passie, M.D.
Laurentius Publishers: 1997

Book Contributions

"A History of the Use of Psilocybin in Psychotherapy"
in *Teonanacatl: Sacred Mushroom of Visions*
by Ralph Metzner, Ph.D.
Park Street Press: 2005

"Contemporary Psychedelic Therapy: An Overview"
in *Psychedelic Medicine: New Evidence for Hallucinogenic Substances as Treatments*, Vol. 1
edited by Michael Winkelman, Ph.D., and Thomas B. Roberts, Ph.D.
Praeger Publishers: 2007

(see References for additional works by Torsten Passie)